P9-CFG-606

Acclaim for *Game Over*

"Most consciences are not as loud, as funny, as entertaining, or as right as often as Dave Zirin, the unquiet conscience of all our games. If you're an owner, fear him. If you're a fan, damn it, listen to him. This is authentic American journalism in a tradition that goes back to William Lloyd Garrison, except funnier, and with fewer civil wars."

—Charles P. Pierce, author of *Idiot America:*
How Stupidity Became a Virtue in the Land of the Free

"There are fresh voices, and there are *fresh* voices. No one approaches sports like Dave Zirin—with genuine love and respect, but also with a kind of X-ray vision that cuts through all of the layers of hype and hypocrisy. *Game Over* is a book that no thinking sports fan can afford to miss."

—Jonathan Mahler, author of *Ladies and Gentlemen, the Bronx Is Burning*

"Zirin has done a remarkable job presenting the complexities and nuances that entwine the worlds of sports and politics. If the majority of athletes and the general public don't challenge the malignant pressures of politics and corporations in sports, we are all diminished."

—Mary Tillman, mother of Pat Tillman and
author of *Boots on the Ground by Dusk*

"*Game Over* tackles head-on various issues of the politics within sports. Zirin's writings are insightful and thought-provoking—and they challenge a conventional mind-set that attempts to cover certain realities and ignore them out of existence."   —Etan Thomas, eleven-year NBA player and author of
Fatherhood: Rising to the Ultimate Challenge

"For novel and insightful sports commentary by one of the country's experts, I recommend *Game Over* with the enthusiasm of a sports fan."

—Nancy Hogshead-Makar, professor of law, senior director of
advocacy at Women's Sports Foundation, and Olympic champion

ALSO BY DAVE ZIRIN

The John Carlos Story:
The Sports Moment That Changed the World

Bad Sports:
How Owners Are Ruining the Games We Love

A People's History of Sports in the United States:
250 Years of Politics, Protest, People, and Play

Welcome to the Terrordome:
The Pain, Politics, and Promise of Sports

Muhammad Ali Handbook

What's My Name, Fool?
Sports and Resistance in the United States

GAME OVER

How Politics Has Turned the Sports World Upside Down

Dave Zirin

THE NEW PRESS

NEW YORK
LONDON

Game Over contains a wealth of new material. It also draws heavily
on my columns over the last three years, published in *The Nation,*
The Progressive, SLAM Magazine, and sportsillustrated.com.
It was only after looking back at them that I thought
that something bigger was happening
in the world of sports.

© 2013 by Dave Zirin
All rights reserved.
No part of this book may be reproduced, in any form,
without written permission from the publisher.

Requests for permission to reproduce selections
from this book should be mailed to: Permissions Department,
The New Press, 38 Greene Street, New York, NY 10013.

Published in the United States by The New Press, New York, 2013
Distributed by Perseus Distribution

ISBN 978-1-59558-815-9 (pbk.)
ISBN 978-1-59558-842-5 (e-book)
CIP data available

The New Press publishes books that promote and enrich public discussion and
understanding of the issues vital to our democracy and to a more equitable world.
These books are made possible by the enthusiasm of our readers; the support
of a committed group of donors, large and small; the collaboration of our many
partners in the independent media and the not-for-profit sector; booksellers, who
often hand-sell New Press books; librarians; and above all by our authors.

www.thenewpress.com

Composition by dix!
This book was set in Fairfield LH Light

Printed in the United States of America

4   6   8   10   9   7   5   3

To John Wesley Carlos, never scared to stand strong

I heard Jim Brown once say the gladiator can't change Rome.
I love Jim Brown. But I disagree. I'll die trying, my brother.
—Arian Foster, NFL Pro Bowl running back

Contents

Acknowledgments

This book doesn't get written without the remarkable work of everyone at The New Press, particularly Azzurra Cox, Marc Favreau, and Ellen Adler. It also doesn't get written without all the support at *The Nation* magazine, *The Progressive*, *SLAM*, the Media Education Foundation, Haymarket Books, and Edge of Sports Radio.

But in the end, nothing gets done without the patience and support of my family, especially Sasha, Jake, and my intergalactic partner, Michele. Lastly, thanks to all the rebel athletes, fans, sports writers, and individuals who seized the last three years and showed the world that politics is not a spectator sport.

Foreword: Scribes and Superheroes

I suspect that Dave Zirin is a superhero. No, I haven't seen him dip in a phone booth in street clothes and emerge in spandex and a cape. But I've witnessed him dropping his rhetorical hammer like Thor on some unsuspecting soul who didn't know that, when it comes to emotions, Dave is in a mixed marriage: his genial spirit is wedded for life to ferocious political resistance.

I still can't quite figure out which superhero he most resembles. It's largely his fault because he routinely goes off script. He's exuberantly subversive. Dave overturns the virtues of our comic book leaders clad in latex and leather. And he often reverses the moral and the magic of the story.

It's only right to begin in Gotham since Zirin's daring work yanks the covers off the real villains of sports who live in a plush but poisonous world of their making. Commissioner Gordon signals his need for help fighting crime by beaming to Batman a shaft of light in the sky.

Zirin's version of Batman is a bit more jarring because he turns the behavior of Gotham's most diligent protector upside down. Our journalistic crusader unmasks hypocrisy in the world of sports. He signals unsportsmanlike conduct by high-ranking officials who sometimes don't play fair. And he shines a bright analytical light on players getting the shaft from baseball commissioner Bud Selig and basketball commissioner David Stern.

Perhaps Dave is Spider-Man, bitten by the eight-legged insect whose name he bears and whose traits he absorbs: spinning webs, crawling on buildings, and swinging from rooftops. Zirin frees us from webs of deception spun about larger-than-life figures at Penn State and Cowboys Stadium. He scales massive structures of deceit about what goes on behind the scenes in every sport from soccer to hockey. And he swings from high theory to pop culture in bringing bad guys and bullies to justice, at least on the page.

Maybe Dave is an anti-superhero who leaves the tights and gloves at home and does his greatest damage as Peter Parker, Bruce Wayne, or Clark Kent—as the guy who looks least likely to deliver a gut punch to the establishment because he looks just like them. He dons no masks; his only weapons are the words he wields like a weight lifted or—better yet—imposed like a cudgel or a baton.

Dave Zirin is a guy who sees the heroic in unexpected places. He's a man who asks tough questions. He's a journalist who uses humor to expose the horrors we so easily overlook. He's a thinker who turns to vital voices that aren't often heard from in the world of sports. And he's an irreverent fan who lampoons the pieties of the testosterone elite.

Take his appearance on a recent episode of ESPN's highly regarded show *Outside the Lines*. While discussing the wild enthusiasm that has greeted the arrival in Washington, D.C., of Heisman Trophy winner Robert Griffin III (affectionately dubbed "RG3"), Zirin acknowledges the glee the Washington Redskins quarterback has generated while slyly getting in a zinger against bigotry. He offers lessons on history and politics to boot.

"Washington, D.C., is a transient town," Dave declares. "It's a town where a lot of people live for a short period of time. And for decades the only thing that has bound this town together as one entity has been Washington, D.C., football."

Note the name of the Washington, D.C., football team wasn't mentioned by Zirin the first time out of the chute. Sometimes it's what's *not* said that speaks the loudest.

"For the last twenty years, this team has been a national embarrassment, and certainly a local embarrassment. And even though that's been the case over the last twenty years—even though FedEx Field, where they play, was ranked by *ESPN* magazine as the twenty-eighth best stadium in the NFL out of thirty-two teams—it's still the third most valuable NFL franchise in the league. That says something about the passion people have for it. And now with RG3, it is like a Redskins inferno here."

Interesting choice of words for sure. Inferno comes from the Latin term for hell, but there's more to the word than its etymology. *Inferno* is the first book of the epic poem *The Divine Comedy,* a classic of Western literature penned by Dante Alighieri. The most relevant issue for our purposes is the association of the Redskins with hell—the hell of losing, the hell of struggle, the hell of troubling nomenclature. That sneaky Dave has hot metaphors and fiery insinuations. And there's more where that flamed from.

"If RG3 held a press conference tomorrow, and said, 'Look, I love this team, I love this town, but I feel like Redskins is a racist name and I'd like to rename the team the Washington Subway Sandwiches,' people might do it! That's how much people love this guy!"

Dave gets a lot done in one statement. He nods to RG3's huge popularity. He highlights the racist shadow on the team's name. He gently nudges the franchise quarterback to use his influence to stamp out vestiges of intolerance. And he even sinks a humorous bite into the commercialization of athletics by alluding to one of RG3's most prominent endorsement deals. (Move over, Jared.)

But he isn't finished. After admitting that Redskins owner Dan Snyder hasn't always been a source of inspiration for the region, Dave concedes Snyder's positive role in feeding the capitol's football obsession.

"The guy has built a lot of goodwill for the team, particularly in Prince George's County, where the Washington Redskins play." Those who know that Prince George's is the wealthiest African American majority county in America know where Dave is heading.

"There really is, I think, in terms of tailgating, no better place. The stadium might be twenty-eighth out of thirty-two, but the passion that people bring is unbelievable. And I have to say, in a town that is very segregated in terms of black and white, you go tailgating at FedEx Field, and it's a remarkably integrated environment. Actually, it's a window into the promise of what this city can be."

That's vintage Zirin: throwing a curve of history over the home plate of sports media and striking out the political ignorance that keeps swinging for the fences of racial amnesia. Or to stick with football, Dave audibles like a poised Peyton Manning at the line of political scrimmage, he reads the blitzes of social denial that attempt to sack the truth, and he tosses a touchdown of radical analysis over the outstretched arms of the defenders of the status quo. That may sound hokey alright, but when bigotry is often outfitted with patriotic garb, the hokey may be downright heroic. And few are as heroic as Dave Zirin in helping us to understand what's at stake in the games we watch and play.

Game Over has a simple but bracing premise: that politics and sports are hitched, for better and worse. As with religion, a lot of folk believe that sport is, and should be, exempt from politics, that it is shielded from questions of justice, equality, and opportunity. Dave Zirin patiently but persistently destroys that myth and hammers at the underlying truth: social, cultural, and racial issues haunt our fields and courts of play as remorselessly as they stalk our national and global lives beyond the arena.

What we think about immigration in America has a huge impact, for instance, on major league baseball, especially since nearly 30 percent of its players are Latino, up from just 13 percent twenty years ago. What impact could the ethnic makeup of baseball possibly have on the game? It might make a difference where the All-Star Game is played—especially if, as in 2011, the destination for the annual display of the game's brightest stars was Arizona, which had recently passed the notorious Support Our Law Enforcement and Safe Neighborhoods Act (SB 1070). That nasty piece of legislation took direct aim at immigrants and empowered the police to conduct a witch hunt for those who are illegally mooching off "our" culture and supposedly sucking the blood from our vital democracy with their vampiric presence.

Zirin, however, exposes the dirt beneath the American carpet of sport. He explores the cowardice of baseball commissioner Selig in refusing, despite reasonable protest, to move the All-Star Game from a state that gave bigotry a license to mock the lives of more than a quarter of baseball's players. He shows how basketball's Phoenix Suns signaled their solidarity with Latinos and their outrage at "anti-immigrant hysteria" by taking to the court in their "Los Suns" jerseys. A small gesture, yes, but a loaded one, too, that seemed to say: if the gravity of the legislation's assault on our common humanity is lost in political translation, then the grammar of our empathy should be made plain as we spell out our allegiance to Latinos.

Zirin also cites the Phoenix Suns' principled stand against homophobia in a blistering critique of how sexual anxieties and prejudices have shaped our expectations of men and women in sport. Men have to make sure that, as the hip-hop slogan states it, there is "no homo" in their routinely rowdy gestures of male bonding: patting butts, showering together, and falling to the floor or field locked up like eager lovers. That stuff is fine as long as the masculine bonding on display is clearly for heterosexual purposes.

As for the fairer sex—the one mostly unfairly treated—it's not enough that women can play; they also have to look pretty and recognizably feminine as they sweat, grunt, and compete. We have to be sure that lesbians aren't lurking in our gyms—though, it appears, it's just fine if they're parading through our heterosexual fantasies of ménages à trois.

Of course the feminine ideal can have an odd and dispiriting racial angle too: when Gabby Douglas won gold at the Olympics as the first black person to snag the top medal for individual all-around gymnastics performance, some black folk took to Twitter to excoriate the pint-size princess for her hair being unkempt as she fried big athletic fish rather than frying her curls. Black self-hatred aside, this peculiar response was thick with gender bias: are any number of black male athletes taken to task for their follicular correctness as they grunt their way toward their goals? Ben Wallace, anyone?

To be sure, race and racism have made more than cameo appearances in the world of sports. Jackie Robinson famously defeated the color line in baseball, and Joe Louis punched his way to American heroism when he bested Max Schmeling in the ring and delivered decisive blows to prejudice beyond the canvas. Those cases were easier to identify—and easier to identify with. All but the most brutal racist can admit that bigotry was wrong and should have had no place in American sport.

But complicated racial views of more recent vintage are dicier: there are no clear-cut heroes and villains.

That may be misstating things. Better to say that the way race plays out in contemporary sports has by shades and degrees gotten a lot more slippery and in some cases more subtle; explicit racial prejudice may have prevailed in the past, but today's racial hierarchy is enforced, and endorsed, by folk who in earlier epochs looked like saviors and heroes.

Zirin adroitly dissects these issues in his discussion of the 2011 lockout of NBA basketball players by the league, led by Commissioner Stern. Most of the players are black, while most of the owners and the commissioner are white. When they went up against the owners, black players, as rich as they are, were, relatively speaking, like so many Davids confronting white billionaire Goliaths. Add to the mix Stern's solid pedigree as a liberal, plus evidence of his paternalism and condescension—he remarked on the players' "inability to understand" the financial woes of team owners—and the result is, well, liberal paternalism and, whether intended or not, racial hierarchy and inequality.

Game Over is refreshing because it takes on racism and a host of other ills with moral clarity and straight talk. Zirin's astute analysis got me to thinking how most conversations about race and sports these days happen at side angles draped in cryptic speech. When LeBron James took his talents to South Beach, the fans in Cleveland went berserk. That's understandable given how much athletes are deified in the culture and how the masses project their muscular fantasies onto their chiseled bodies. (Okay, so Prince Fielder's generous girth doesn't exactly qualify him for *ESPN* magazine's annual body issue, but his extraordinary skills and lucrative contract make him an object of desire nonetheless.) But it's also telling that so much of the anger unleashed on LeBron wasn't simply about a hometown hero decamping for newer vineyards as he left behind the bitter whines of his jilted lovers. The charge that LeBron publicly humiliated his hometown and his team by announcing his decision on a nationally televised special is largely unconvincing. Everything else he did was equally large and dramatic, perhaps even theatric, and no one was complaining then, except the towns and teams he left in his athletic dust. Besides, for nearly two years before he left Cleveland, James had cameras and microphones stuck in his face everywhere he went, whether to the cleaners or the bathroom, asking what he would do. It made sense to tell everyone at the same time. No, he shouldn't have told team owner Dan Gilbert his decision beforehand, or else he would have ruined the moment and spoiled the surprise as surely as he stewed in undeclared racial resentment afterward.

The notion of a black athlete being free to declare his intentions to pursue his dreams where he wanted without asking permission of a white owner reeked too heavily of the sort of independence that in the past was read as racial betrayal. James did nothing illegal or immoral. He exercised a right of choice that is usually at the owner's or team's discretion: when and under what terms a player would go and where he would end up. Since all but one of the league's owners is white, and 80 percent of the players are black, the racial ledger unavoidably finds a bottom line in race. Had James announced he was remaining in Cleveland, the hero's garland and the saint's halo may very well have been his. A parade with floats may have greeted him instead of the burning jersey and the hanging in effigy.

These are the kinds of thoughts that *Game Over* provokes. And that's merely the tip of the iceberg. Zirin wrestles with the Penn State child molestation scandal: he contrasts, then connects, our reverence for figures like legendary football coach Joe Paterno on the gridiron with the heaving injustices carried out by assistant coach Jerry Sandusky in the showers. Zirin untangles the gnarled logic of paying NCAA coaches big money, including millions in endorsements from corporate behemoths like Nike, while the athletes who carry the financial well-being of the university on their backs barely scrape by on conditional scholarships. He's equally smart about the impact of the Arab Spring on soccer and the sordid collusion of big capital and political repression on the Olympics.

Dave Zirin makes us understand that "whether we see ourselves as sports fans or not, we all have a stake in understanding why the sports page is insufficient for understanding sports." Seeing the world through his eyes is a revelation; reading his poetic prose as he grapples with the politics of sports is exhilarating. In a time when many athletes—and their scribes as well—have been warned and weaned away from politics, Dave Zirin brilliantly shows us how the bullpen and the bully pulpit have a lot in common. In my book, with all apologies to Shaq and Dwight Howard, that makes him the real Superman.

—Michael Eric Dyson

GAME OVER

Pre-Game

Don't look back. Something might be gaining on you.

—Satchel Paige

In March 2012, the Miami Heat chose to put down their basketballs and put on their hoodies. As a team, they stood shoulder to shoulder and did what we are told athletes no longer do: made a conscious political stand for justice. The entire Heat roster—from stars LeBron James, Dwyane Wade, and Chris Bosh to South Dakota's Mike Miller to the nearly forty-year-old reserve Juwan Howard—stood as one for seventeen-year-old Trayvon Martin, who had been recently killed by armed self-appointed "neighborhood watch leader" George Zimmerman. While Martin's killer had a nine-millimeter, the teenager had nothing but a pack of Skittles and a can of Arizona iced tea in his pocket. Trayvon was wearing a hoodie when he died, which some pundits in their infinite wisdom believed made him "suspicious" and worthy of being pursued.[1]

Of all the teams in the league, the Heat were the most shocking yet also most appropriate to step up and be heard. It was shocking because the Heat are often painted as being a collection of prima donnas, as allegedly superficial as the town they call home. It was also appropriate because this was Trayvon's favorite team, and he was killed after leaving his house during halftime of the NBA All-Star Game, where he was watching James and Wade perform.

Given the outrage over Trayvon Martin's death, particularly in southern Florida, the Heat's powerful gesture hardly came out of the blue. What may be surprising for many fans is that "the King" himself, LeBron James, drove the effort. The March 2012 team photo was reportedly James's idea and was first posted to his personal Twitter account with the hashtag #WeWantJustice.[2]

James later said, "It was very emotional, an emotional day for all of us. Taking that picture, we're happy that we're able to shed light on the situation that we feel is unjust."[3] His teammate Wade commented to the Associated Press, "This situation hit home for me because last Christmas, all my oldest son wanted as a gift was hoodies. So when I heard about this a week ago, I thought of my sons. I'm speaking up because I feel it's necessary that we get past the stereotype of young, black men."[4]

Since he was a teenager, "King James" has been pegged as potentially the greatest basketball player alive. He's a Fortune 500 company with legs and, thus far, has a very carefully crafted apolitical image. He is also someone who was raised by a single mother in Akron, Ohio, at times so poor that they were living in a car. He has everything, as well as memories of having had nothing. Perhaps this is why he once said that his dream is to be "a global icon like Muhammad Ali."[5] We've rarely seen evidence of his efforts to achieve this dream, but the hoodie photo could be a result of the Ali in him straining to be heard.

At the Heat's home game the following Friday night, James and several of his teammates took the floor with messages such as "RIP Trayvon Martin" and "We want justice" scrawled on their sneakers. Their actions inspired others across the NBA. Players spanning the gamut—from stars, like Steve Nash and Carmelo Anthony, to less famous jocks, such as Will Bynum and Brandon Knight—spoke out to raise awareness. Anthony, the high-profile star of the New York

Knicks, changed his own Twitter picture to show him in a hoodie with "I am Trayvon Martin" superimposed over his body.

Detroit Pistons center Greg Monroe explained to the *Detroit Free Press* why so many players wanted to say something. "These kids come from the same neighborhoods we walked—or worse. And we see the same news everybody sees. When we turn on CNN, we don't have a special CNN channel. When we get pulled over, there's no special millionaire cops. We're just paid to play basketball."[6]

To put it a different way, athletes aren't cartoon characters or robots. They are a part of this world. We are often told that today's athletes have no stake, as their forebears did, in fighting for change. At one time, athletes, particularly athletes of color and women athletes, had a self-interest in broader struggles against discrimination, but no longer. The argument goes that we are now somehow a "postracial, postpolitical" society. But while there are more people than ever telling us that the world has changed, injustice, discrimination, and inequality of opportunity still rule the land.

In the real world, any change at all has been incremental and hard-won. In the sports world, there's been a different kind of change and it couldn't be more dramatic. Over the last thirty years, the athletic-industrial complex has transformed itself into a trillion-dollar, global entity. One way it's done this is by making its product and its players as explicitly apolitical as possible. From Peyton Manning to Derek Jeter to Danica Patrick, the dominant message projected by athletes has been that it's far more important to be a brand than an individual, and that a modern jock should never sacrifice commercial concerns for political principle. This credo echoes Jesse Owens, the great Olympic star, who once said, "The only time the black fist has significance is when there's money inside."[7]

ESPN, twenty-four-hour talk radio, and a seemingly bottomless appetite for distraction have exploded the size of our sports

world—and its profits—into the stratosphere. In conjunction with
this expansion, politics has also been actively discouraged by management and slammed by sports columnists. Legendary sportscaster
Howard Cosell toward the end of his life dubbed it rule number
one of "the jockocracy": sports and politics just don't mix.[8]

Yet over the last several years, the specter of politics has been
haunting sports. Cosell's Golden Rule has been repeatedly and flagrantly breached. More athletes are speaking out across the political spectrum as a series of revolutions, occupations, and protests
has defined the global landscape. The real world is gaining on the
sports world and the sports world is starting to look over its shoulder. This book explores how and why this is taking place. As I hope
to show, whether we see ourselves as sports fans or not, we all have
a stake in understanding why the sports page is insufficient for understanding sports.

The Wall Between Sports and Politics Is Breached

On Cinco de Mayo in 2010, the NBA's Phoenix Suns went where
no American sports team had gone before. In their playoff game
against the San Antonio Spurs, the squad took to the court wearing jerseys that read simply "Los Suns." They were coming out as
one against Arizona's Senate Bill 1070, which critics said would
codify racial profiling by criminalizing anyone suspected of being
an undocumented immigrant. This was the first time in U.S. sports
history that an entire team—from owner to general manager to
players—had expressed any kind of unified political stance. This
audacious move by the Suns was perhaps the most publicized
moment of a low-frequency sea change in the world of sports.

There were the members of the Green Bay Packers who stood—
and continue to stand—behind the workers of Wisconsin under attack by the state's Governor Scott Walker.

There were the soccer players and clubs in the Middle East who played a leading role in the Arab Spring and, with unprecedented impact, are helping shape their revolutions.

There were the two NFL players—Pro Bowler Brendon Ayanbadejo and New Orleans Saints Super Bowl hero Scott Fujita—who spoke out in favor of LGBT marriage equality in the fall of 2009. (They have been joined by basketball star Steve Nash, New England Patriot Rob Gronkowski, New York Giant Michael Strahan, New York Ranger Sean Avery, Charles Barkley, Michael Irvin, and other players willing to speak out on what was recently a taboo locker room subject.)

Other political explosions have recently detonated inside the world of sports. Labor lockouts in the NFL and NBA have brought a taste of the broader economic crisis that provoked the Occupy movement into this supposedly privileged space. The explosive child-molestation charges at Penn State University and broader issues of corruption in the NCAA have raised political questions that speak to the very role we expect our universities to play. College athletes in the "revenue-producing" sports of football and basketball have signed petitions to form organizations and unshackle themselves from an ugly, utterly corrupt system.

Discussions about Tim Tebow, Jeremy Lin, Caster Semenya, and many others have created a buzz and a dialogue beyond the confines of sports radio. When Boston Bruins goalie Tim Thomas turned down the team's invitation to go to the White House after they won the 2011 Stanley Cup, he wasn't content with quiet protest and instead posted a Tea Party–influenced monologue on his Facebook page. When Joel Ward, a black player for the Washington Capitals, scored a playoff-clinching goal on Thomas in 2012, the racist bile on Twitter was so intense that players and the media felt compelled to respond.

The more recent political eruptions are in many respects a hangover from the 2008 elections, when an unprecedented number of athletes went public in support of Barack Obama's candidacy and the efforts to elect an African American president. Some of the most commercially successful—and therefore some of the most commercially vulnerable—jocks became involved in the campaign. LeBron James wore Obama T-shirts to games and all-star players like Baron Davis and Chauncey Billups vocally supported his candidacy. Boston Celtics star Kevin Garnett wore sneakers with "Vote for Change" scrawled on their sides. Then Denver Nuggets star Carmelo Anthony pledged that he would score forty-four points in a game in honor of the future forty-fourth president (he only scored twenty-eight, which was, one can assume, not a tribute to Woodrow Wilson). When Billups was asked if he was concerned that his public support of Obama would hurt his endorsement chances, he said, "Like I give a shit."

As it turns out, a whole new generation of "Jocks for Justice" is rejecting the yoke of apathy and speaking out about the world. NBA players like Nash, Etan Thomas, and Joakim Noah, as well as NFL players Scott Fujita and Adalius Thomas, raised objections against the U.S. war in Iraq. Even Ultimate Fighting champion Jeff "the Snowman" Monson took to distributing antiwar pamphlets on his way to the "Octagon" and was arrested protesting at the 2008 Republican National Convention. As Martina Navratilova said to *Sports Illustrated* in 2008, "It's like athletes have woken up to what actors and musicians have known forever: I have this amazing platform—why not use it?"[9]

These small acts of solidarity may seem negligible—but they matter. Whether we like it or not, athletes are role models; it's worth asking, then, what are they in fact modeling?

While not every athlete acts like his life's ambition off the playing field is to be featured on *MTV Cribs,* the media loves to highlight the salacious and scandalous. It's not just the worst examples, like football player Ben Roethlisberger, who was investigated twice for rape, or Adam "Pac Man" Jones getting in trouble with the law at "gentleman's clubs." As a rule, the pro athletes who engage in the most mindless conspicuous consumption are the ones who tend to be highlighted.

If, instead of modeling crass materialism, more athletes chose to display a broader sense of community awareness—no matter the issue or politics—we'd all be better off. Even when I personally disagree with the politics of an athlete (see Tim Tebow), the mere fact that he is saying anything has the potential to initiate a dialogue more full and involving than anything we get from Capitol Hill.

Having athletes risk their prime perch in society for the greater good also becomes a kind of weather vane, a crackling signal that we have entered a new era. In 1968, political struggle was part of the oxygen of the sports world. The people and the games we watched were shaped by the struggles in the streets.

In a time that has seen revolts from the Middle East to the Midwest, we can look at the facts on the ground and note that the citadel of American sports has also been breached. The apolitical 1990s were dubbed the "vacation from history." Well, vacation is over and history has returned with a vengeance—severe enough to cross the moat and enter the locker room.

Why are more athletes speaking out? Some point to social media as a critical delivery system for a generation of athletes who don't trust "old school" reporters. Hundred-and-forty-character bursts and Facebook posts offer the ability to speak without a filter directly to fans.

Another theory is that players are now actually encouraged, for commercial reasons, to "define their own brand." I spoke at a seminar for NBA rookies where the dominant theme was how players could distinguish themselves and create a memorable persona for their audience. Just repeating clichés by rote, like "We give 150 percent and play one game at a time," is now seen as a liability. But the most compelling reason is simply, as Greg Monroe said, that the world is changing and athletes are a part of that world.

But speaking out still has a cost. We saw this in May 2011, after al-Qaeda leader and "9/11 mastermind" Osama bin Laden was killed by U.S. Navy SEALs. In the aftermath of his assassination, the sports world embraced the public eruption of patriotism. From the spontaneous cheers of forty thousand fans in Philadelphia to amped "Military Appreciation Night" celebrations at stadiums around the country, the sports world exulted in the euphoria of bin Laden's dramatic demise.

Yet some athletes dared to buck the trend—and, in the process, learned a tough lesson about the limits of free speech in the jockocracy. Chris Douglas-Roberts, former Memphis basketball all-American and Milwaukee Buck, responded to bin Laden's death with a litany of reasons why he wasn't joining the party, tweeting, among other things, "It took 919,967 deaths to kill that one guy. It took 10 years & 2 Wars to kill that guy. It cost us (USA) roughly $1,188,263,000,000 to kill that guy. But we winning though. Haaaa. (Sarcasm)."

Profanity, threats, and the general belief that he was "stupid" and a "moron" who should shut his "dumb [expletive] mouth" because he is "not intelligent" came rolling in. Douglas-Roberts tried to hit back, tweeting: "What I'm sayin has nothing to do with 9/11 or that guy (Bin Laden). I still feel bad for the 9/11 families but I feel EQUALLY bad for the war families. . . . People are telling me to get out of America now b/c I'm against MORE INNOCENT people dying everyday? B/c I'm against a 10 year WAR? Whatever happened to our freedom of speech? What I've learned tonight, athletes shouldn't have perspectives. But I don't care. We feel certain ways about things TOO."[10]

Rashard Mendenhall, the Pro Bowl running back for the Pittsburgh Steelers, raised eyebrows even higher with his comments, writing, "[For] those of you who said you want to see Bin Laden burn in hell and piss on his ashes, I ask how would God feel about your heart? . . . What kind of person celebrates death?" Mendenhall then took it further and voiced his doubts about the official story of the 9/11 attacks, causing *Sports Illustrated's* senior football writer Don Banks to write a piece titled "Mendenhall Just the Latest NFL Player to Spout Utter Nonsense."[11]

The outrage intensified to the point where Steelers president Art Rooney II, a big money bundler for President Obama and the U.S. ambassador to Ireland, had to actually issue a formal statement about a tweet, writing, "I have not spoken with Rashard so it is hard to explain or even comprehend what he meant with his recent Twitter comments. The entire Steelers' organization is very proud of the job our military personnel have done and we can only hope this leads to our troops coming home soon."[12]

Whether or not you supported some or all the wars of the last decade, it should be clear that the guardians of jock culture are trying to teach athletes a lesson: you have signed away your right to have an opinion beyond your choice of sneaker or sports drink. This is something that runs very deeply in the marrow of our sports world: the idea that athletes, particularly athletes of color, should just "shut up and play."

Douglas-Roberts and Mendenhall also unintentionally exposed the most bizarre contradiction of this no-politics rule. Players are strongly encouraged by management, family, and the media to follow the rules and "never talk politics"—but whether we choose to acknowledge it or not, a politically charged atmosphere pervades all of professional sports. I don't just say that because I live in a town where people root for a team called the Redskins. I say so because at every sporting event we are encouraged to collectively celebrate the displays of nationalism, patriotism, and military might that festoon every corner. In addition, the politics of big business and big sponsorship deals saturate sports arenas. At one point, baseball owners wanted to put ads for *Spider-Man 2* on every second base, and only backed away when fans erupted in outrage. Even college football players, so-called amateurs, are trussed in ads to a degree that would shame NASCAR. If only the owners of pro sports teams could create a red, white, and blue beer, they might collectively keel over in joy.

But throughout history, we've also seen athletes take this setup and stand it on its head. This has happened when they have used their exalted, hypercommercialized platform to say something about the world and then dare those in power to shut them up. There is a reason we associate people like Jackie Robinson with the civil rights movement; Muhammad Ali with the 1960s; Billie Jean King with the women's movement; or 1968 Olympian Tom Waddell, the founder of the Gay Games, with LGBT rights. This history indicates that sports is never just a spectacle—that it has a potential to tap into sentiments for social change.

Our sports culture shapes societal attitudes, relationships, and power arrangements. It is where cultural meanings—our very notions of who we are and how we see each other, not only as Americans but also as individuals—play out. It frames the ways in which we understand and discuss issues of gender, race, and class. And, as ever, it is crucial for understanding how these norms and power structures have been negotiated, struggled with, and resisted.

These are important questions, and they're questions the guardians of sport don't want asked. This book will ask those questions. This book aims to make sense of all the noise that the boosters and shills in the athletic-industrial complex are trying, and failing, to ignore. We are going to look at all the ways sports, politics, revolution, and reaction have collided in recent years and try to understand if the political messages that flow through sports are, in fact, a canary in the coal mine for all of us. I hope to show that the stakes couldn't be higher.

· 1 ·

Occupy the Sports World

The year 2011 was defined by revolutions in the Middle East and radical Occupy movements across the globe. While "the Protester" stole the cover of *Time* magazine as its "Person of the Year," the sports world was experiencing a level of political and economic upheaval the likes of which we haven't seen in more than four decades. In 1968, as war, violence, and revolt gripped the world, currents of social and political change found an unmistakable echo in the world of sports. The year 1968 saw Muhammad Ali—banned from boxing and out on appeal after receiving a five-year prison sentence for avoiding the draft—give two hundred speeches on college campuses and proclaim to his audiences, "Keep asking me how long on Vietnam I sing this song, I ain't got no quarrel with them Vietcong." It saw the greatest stars, like Bill Russell, Jim Brown, and Lew Alcindor, embrace politics without shame. And if there was one moment that crystallized not only 1968 but an entire era of resistance against war and racism, it was when Tommie Smith and John Carlos raised their black-gloved fists to the sky and brought the revolt to the most unlikely of places: the Olympic Games. Bill Russell said after their medal-stand protest that his only problem with their actions was that he didn't think of it first.

Just as in 1968, the spirit of radical change shaped 2011. A wave of revolutions and revolts were felt from the Middle East to the Midwest. This was the year of #Occupy, and nothing is the same as it was before. And, just as in 1968, this spirit has reverberated in the world of sports.

2011 saw owners lock out their players in the National Football League and National Basketball Association. While both were painted by the media as a struggle "between billionaires and millionaires," something deeper was taking place. Both were triggered because of attempts by owners to shift the burden of their leagues' economic crisis onto their players, making them pay for the poor decisions and planning of those at the top. This is essentially the same dynamic that pushed protesters into the streets of Tunisia, Egypt, Greece, London, and Madison, Wisconsin. Both sports lockouts also resulted in very different outcomes, the result, I will argue, of the two groups' drastically different approaches to the broader social movements that are defining this moment in time.

But the year's dazzling collisions of sports and politics were foretold in January, when the Green Bay Packers won the 2011 Super Bowl. In a thrilling game, during which the Packers beat the Steelers 31–25 behind a three-hundred-yard performance by Packers QB Aaron Rodgers, the show's announcers Joe Buck and Troy Aikman made a brazen decision: not once did they mention the Packers' unique ownership structure. Often, the Super Bowl includes shots of the two teams' owners fretting like neurotic Julius Caesars in their luxury boxes. But the Packers are a community-run nonprofit, owned in 2011 by each and every one of 112,000 fans. This state of affairs provides peculiar advantages no other NFL team shares. The Packers can never be moved to another city. Their stadium, Lambeau Field, will never be torn down and replaced with a 1.5-billion-dollar monument to corporate welfare. They give 60 percent of their concession profits to local charities. When they need a cash infusion, they sell more stock instead of passing on the tax burden wholesale onto the entire populace. And, perhaps most importantly in Wisconsin, beer prices at Lambeau Field stand at roughly half of that at the average stadium. Rather than celebrate these facts, Fox buried them.

With the NFL lockout looming, however, this was hardly surprising. After all, the team from Green Bay stands as a living, breathing example that if you take the profit motive out of sports, you can get more than a team to be proud of: you get a Super Bowl champion. They demonstrate that pro-sports owners are about as superfluous and outdated as having your own Betamax. There are more than a few fans in more than a few cities who would pony up for some stock shares if it meant that they wouldn't be held up for a publicly funded stadium, wouldn't have to worry about the team's leaving town, or were assured that their team's owner would be sent packing, leaving sports decisions to those who actually know something about sports and don't think their paycheck and years of watching television have made them into an expert. (Looking at you, Dan Snyder.)

If the broadcast did not mention Green Bay's unique ownership structure, the people of Wisconsin celebrated it with gusto following their Super Bowl triumph. When Packers head coach Mike McCarthy rallied in front of thousands of Cheeseheads back home in Wisconsin, the Lombardi Trophy in hand, he said, "We're a community-owned football team, so you can see all the fingerprints on our trophy."[1] When Republican governor Scott Walker, at the time recently elected, took the stage after McCarthy, he was audibly booed. But this didn't stop Walker from bathing himself in the team's triumph, slathering himself in their glory. When Walker publicly declared that February was now to be Packers Month, he oozed praise for the franchise, saying, "I congratulate their unprecedented success, and I enthusiastically commend this observance to all citizens."[2]

Just days later, Walker unveiled plans to strip all public workers of collective bargaining rights and dramatically slash the wages and health benefits of every nurse, teacher, and state employee. Then, in advance of any debate over his proposal, Walker warned that the Wisconsin National Guard would be "prepared" to meet any resistance with "whatever the governor, their commander-in-chief, might call for."[3] Considering that the state of Wisconsin had not called in the National Guard since 1886, these bizarre threats did more than raise polite, Midwestern eyebrows. They provoked rage.

Robin Eckstein, a former Wisconsin National Guard member, told the Huffington Post, "Maybe the new governor doesn't understand yet—but the National Guard is not his own personal intimidation force to be mobilized to quash political dissent."[4]

I was in Madison the week when the marches started, and it was remarkable to see them mature from set-piece demonstrations to something as aggressive, grassroots, and intense as anything this country has seen in decades. The week started on Valentine's Day, when the teachers' union held professionally printed signs that read, "Governor Walker: Have a Heart!" I remember thinking that this, frankly, bordered on lame. But soon the students walked out of their classes and the teachers called in sick. The feeder marches followed, converging on the capitol from points all over Madison. I ran from one to another, floored by what felt like hundreds of thousands of people, ages six to sixty, loud and angry. A slew of signs referred explicitly to the events in the Middle East earlier that year: "If Egypt Can Have Democracy, Why Can't Wisconsin?," and "We Want Governors Not Dictators," and the pithy Mubarak nod: "Hosni Walker."

But what this stunned sportswriter, who has been to his share of demonstrations, found as striking as the amusing signage and angry chants was the sheer number of Packers jackets and hats. If the protesters had pooled their Packers gear, they could have outfitted

Lambeau Field. (I grew up in New York City, and it's difficult to imagine a labor demonstration with masses of workers and students sporting Jets and Giants gear.) It wasn't just hats and jackets on that cold, mercifully snow-free week in February. There were signs on display that read, "Aaron Rodgers is a Union Rep and so am I" and "Scott Walker is a Bears fan." One banner read, "The Packers are run by the people. The Government is run by the rich." I spoke to one teacher who put it perfectly: "Wisconsin is a grassroots kind of state and the Packers are a grassroots team, owned by the fans. . . . Standing for workers' rights is about being a Packers fan. They're one and the same. When we see Walker in a Packers jersey, it feels like an insult."

Fandom is often cited as something that draws energy away from positive struggle for social change. To see Packer Nation propelled by the unique situation of their ownership structure toward activism was remarkable all by itself. Besides, the fact of community ownership means that this is a team whose very existence is a threat not only to NFL owners, but also to the idea espoused by everyone, from Scott Walker to Mitt Romney to Paul Ryan, that the wealthy are untouchable "job creators" to whom we should tip our hat at every opportunity.

But the most extraordinary part of this display wasn't just the symbol of the Super Bowl–winning Packers in the streets of Madison; it was the Packers themselves. Then-current players Brady Poppinga and Jason Spitz and former Packers Curtis Fuller, Chris Jacke, Charles Jordan, Bob Long, and Steve Okoniewski issued the following statement at the height of the Madison demonstrations:

> We know that it is teamwork on and off the field that makes the Packers and Wisconsin great. As a publicly owned team we wouldn't have been able to win the Super Bowl without the support of our fans. It is the same dedication of our

public workers every day that makes Wisconsin run. They are the teachers, nurses, and child care workers who take care of us and our families. But now in an unprecedented political attack Governor Walker is trying to take away their right to have a voice and bargain at work. The right to negotiate wages and benefits is a fundamental underpinning of our middle class. When workers join together it serves as a check on corporate power and helps ALL workers by raising community standards. Wisconsin's long-standing tradition of allowing public sector workers to have a voice on the job has worked for the state since the 1930s. It has created greater consistency in the relationship between labor and management and a shared approach to public work. These public workers are Wisconsin's champions every single day and we urge the Governor and the State Legislature to not take away their rights.[5]

Then, on February 15, NFL Players Association executive director DeMaurice Smith issued his own statement in support of state workers, writing, "The NFL Players Association will always support efforts protecting a worker's right to join a union and collectively bargain. Today, the NFLPA stands in solidarity with its organized labor brothers and sisters in Wisconsin."[6]

Given that the NFLPA was facing a lockout of its own, the opportunity for solidarity was there to be seized. The following week, Charles Woodson, the only Packers player with the profile, respect, and cultural currency to rival Aaron Rodgers, went public with his own support. Woodson is the team's defensive captain, but he's really more than that. A future Hall of Famer, a Heisman Trophy winner at the University of Michigan, an NFL defensive player of the year, and a perennial Pro Bowler, Woodson is, most important, the team's vocal and emotional leader. News that he had voiced his support for the struggle evoked cheers in the capitol and shock waves in the governor's office. The great Woodson, charged with pumping fans up at halftime and making speeches after the game, said during the playoffs, "The President [a Chicago Bears fan] doesn't want to watch us in the Super Bowl? We'll go see him! Say White House on three!"[7]

Woodson is also one of the team's union reps. As the Packer Nation wondered if Chris Jacke was going to be the most high-profile Packer to speak out, Woodson openly proclaimed his solidarity with the then-looming lockout:

> Last week I was proud when many of my current and former teammates announced their support for the working families fighting for their rights in Wisconsin. Today I am honored to join with them. . . . These hardworking people are under an unprecedented attack to take away their basic rights to have a voice and collectively bargain at work. . . . I hope those leading the attack will sit down with Wisconsin's public workers and discuss the problems Wisconsin faces, so that together they can truly move Wisconsin forward.[8]

The Packers' support was not lost on those marching in the streets. Aisha Robertson, a public school teacher from Madison, said to me, "It's great to see Packers join the fight against Walker. Their statement of support shows they stand with us. It gives us inspiration and courage to go and fight peacefully for our most basic rights."

The movement soon moved from protests to recall votes for Governor Walker and several members of the state senate. One of the get-out-the-vote spokespeople was another Packers hero, the retired Gilbert Brown. The beloved defensive lineman, with a girth that could block out the bright winter sun, recorded a highly publicized statement where he said, "Hello, this is Gilbert Brown, defensive lineman for the '97 Super Bowl champion Green Bay Packers, calling on behalf of We Are Wisconsin. . . . I know a little bit about playing defense and right now it is time to defend Wisconsin. We are holding the line, putting our children's education before big corporate tax giveaways. It is up to voters like you to make the difference."[9]

Walker no doubt envisioned conflict when he rolled out his plan to bulldoze the public-sector workers of Wisconsin. But I do not think he foresaw having to go toe-to-toe with the Green Bay Packers. I also do not think he foresaw the other sports union facing a lockout—the National Basketball Players Association—joining against him.

In the NFL lockout, players were facing the prospect of playing more games for less money. NBA players were threatened with steep pay cuts as well as the added possibility of contracting several teams. The NBA had also recently welcomed several owners from the Scott Walker slash-and-burn school of business, like the Cleveland Cavaliers' boss, who is also the CEO of Quicken Loans, "Subprime" Dan Gilbert, and multibillionaire Russian plutocrat Mikhail Prokhorov. When Republican state legislators convened a late-night vote to strip public-sector employees of their rights to collectively bargain without even the pretense of a quorum, that was, for NBA Players Association executive director Billy Hunter, a call to arms. "Last night's vote by the Wisconsin Assembly was an attempt to undermine organized labor and the men and women across the country who depend on their unions for a voice in the workplace," said Hunter. "The NBPA proudly supports our brothers and sisters in Wisconsin and their stand for unequivocal collective bargaining rights."[10]

Hunter has been part of the labor movement for many years. Less expected was the contribution from the Milwaukee Bucks' Keyon Dooling, the team's player rep. "Wisconsin public sector workers tirelessly deliver services on a daily basis to millions of Wisconsin residents," said Dooling. "Wisconsin's workers deserve better than last night's vote. Today, our union stands proudly with our fellow union members throughout the state as they continue their fight."[11]

Dooling, it's worth noting, took a stronger stand than one of the state's leading Democrats, Wisconsin Democratic senator Herb Kohl. Herb Kohl is not-so-incidentally also the owner of the Milwaukee Bucks.

When dealing with periods of profound protest, it always makes sense to turn to those who have been there before. I spoke with Dr. John Carlos, the 1968 Olympian who raised a black-gloved fist at the Mexico City Olympics. John Carlos knows intimately the price that must be paid when athletes speak truth to power, and he believes that these actions on behalf of protesters are more than appropriate: they're righteous. Here is what Dr. Carlos said to me at the time:

> I don't think Governor Walker realizes that workers are the people who built this country and workers are the people who keep the fabric of our communities together. Workers are the people of the grassroots. For him or any political figure to try and cut their wages, take their health care, crush their unions, or subjugate them in any way is just a travesty. . . . I commend what the workers, students, athletes, and all protesters are doing to stand up for their rights and I am with them one thousand percent. Every person from the world of sports with a heart or sense of humanity would say the same.

The NFL Lockout and the "Beauty of Work"

As the NFL lockout wore on, the league's players association closely monitored the fight in Wisconsin. One reason was basic union solidarity. I interviewed DeMaurice Smith, who said,

> I'm proud to sit on the executive council of the AFL-CIO. We share all the same issues that the American people share. We want decent wages. We want a fair pension. . . . The minute that any sports player believes for whatever reason that they are outside the management-labor paradigm you will start to lose ground. Our guys get their fingers broken, their backs broken, their heads concussed, and their knees torn up because they actually put their hands into the ground and work for a living, and I would much rather have them understand and appreciate and frankly embrace the beauty of what it is to work and provide for their family.

By highlighting their labor credentials, it was also easier for the NFL Players Association to explain to the public that this lockout was fundamentally more complex than "millionaires vs. billionaires." As Smith said,

> Our side of the table, the average career for a football player is 3.6 years. It takes you three years and three games in order to get five years of health care coverage when you're done playing. If you play any less than three years you don't get any health care coverage when you retire. If you play three years and three games, you still only get five years . . . so you take a guy who graduates from college at 22, the average career is 3.6 years, let's say he plays four years. Players are retiring at the ripe old age of 26. Five years of health care coverage and

everything after that, every injury you have is a preexisting condition. Try to find insurance for that. So when they say to me, it's a battle between billionaires and millionaires, that's where I start.

Smith went on to relate this struggle to that of people at the bottom of the economic food chain:

> We also try to remind people that if we get locked out, we have thirty thousand people who work in our stadiums. They're locked out. The concession workers and the people who are parking cars in the sleet and the rain for their fourth or fifth job, they're locked out. The bars and the restaurants that rely on football, they're locked out. The families of our players that rely on the health care, no health care. I don't really look at this as a battle between millionaires and billionaires. I look at this as a battle between thirty-two people who can unilaterally shut down our game, and America, who digs it.

The NFL was telling the players to take less money while also pushing for two more games, and the effect was nothing short of radicalizing. These players have former teammates with postconcussive ailments that range from ALS (Lou Gehrig's disease) to depression; from memory loss to impaired motor function. Some are simply unable to pick up their kids or even remember their names. For NFL commissioner Roger Goodell to espouse safety concerns while proposing a longer season and benefits cuts was a shock to their system. It was a wake-up call that the NFL world is run by its own highly dictatorial, even militaristic, code—a code at odds with players who want to have a say in their health, their business, and the quality of their lives.

Given all that was happening from the Middle East to the Midwest, the real world began to bleed into the sports world. Months before the Occupy movement raised questions about the 99 percent's being forced to bail out the 1 percent, this is what Pittsburgh Steelers safety Troy Polamalu said about the NFL lockout:

> I think what the players are fighting for is something bigger. A lot of people think it's millionaires versus billionaires and that's the huge argument. The fact is it's people fighting against big business. The big business argument is "I got the money and I got the power therefore I can tell you what to do." That's life everywhere. I think this is a time when the football players are standing up and saying, "No, no, no, the people have the power."[12]

DeMaurice Smith would refer directly to the revolutions brewing in the Middle East:

> There are some socially and politically significant things occurring in the world that don't have anything to do with the final score. . . . I've just been glued to what's been going on in Egypt and the way in which ordinary people are taking a stand against what they feel is oppression. And let's get it clear, those folks are risking everything to take ownership of what their lives are going to look like. It's the least we can do.[13]

NFL players soon started speaking at local union meetings and rallies, making real efforts at solidarity rarely attempted in the history of sports labor conflicts. The unions welcomed them with open arms. I saw former NFL player Nolan Harrison speak at a strike of Washington, DC, hospital nurses and bring the crowd to cheers. He spoke movingly about his own mother's being a health care worker, linking the lockout to the broader struggle of low-wage workers in an insecure, service-based economy.

The NFLPA fought the lockout in a manner that distinguished them from any sports labor conflict since the days of Curt Flood, the 1960s–70s Major League Baseball star who sacrificed his career to win free agency and refused to be, as he said, "a well-paid slave." The NFLPA regularly took part in forums and press conferences with low-wage stadium workers who would have suffered lost wages if there were no games in the fall of 2011. When I asked Smith if this was aimed at pressuring Goodell and the owners, he responded:

> I don't know if it places pressure on him or not, whether it places pressure on the owners or not, and frankly, I don't care. This is what we do. The business of football means that there's over 150 thousand people who work in [businesses connected to game day during the season]. . . . So to say that we can live, work and operate in a world where we can intellectually or morally divorce ourselves from everything that's going on outside of our circle, you can't, you simply can't.

It was all a far cry from the days of George Meany, the first president of the AFL-CIO, who said, "I have no use for ball players as union men. You'd never see the day when one of those high-priced bozos would honor a picket line set up around the ballpark by the beer vendors, would you?"[14]

The results of a strategy hinging on the issues of health benefits, care for retired players, and connecting with low-wage workers locked out of their jobs by management speak for themselves: the NFLPA's successful effort saw the players travel from a profound disadvantage to a collective bargaining agreement (CBA) that redresses the worst aspects of being labor in the NFL. As part of the league's new ten-year CBA, minimum salaries will go up 10 percent annually for the life of the agreement. Players get a slightly lower percentage of revenues (about 47 percent, down from 50 percent), but they receive 55 percent of future national media revenue, which will mushroom in the years ahead. Teams also now have to spend at least 90 percent of the salary cap on actual salaries. In other words, there isn't just a salary cap, there's a salary floor. In return, rookies need to sign four-year contracts that are scaled at a lower rate. The net effect is that veterans' salaries will go up perhaps quite dramatically, and if players can stay healthy beyond that fourth year, they will be very well compensated.

But there's a catch. If the average career is only 3.4 years, how can players stay healthy enough to reach the big payday? Here is where I think the NFLPA made the most headway. Not only did they beat back the owners' dream of an eighteen-game season, they also negotiated a much less arduous off-season regimen. The off-season program will now be five weeks shorter; there will be more days off, and full-contact practices are going to be greatly curtailed. This will limit not just the wear and tear on players' bodies but also concussions and other brain injuries, which are far more likely to happen during repetitive drills than in games.

And when careers finally do end, players can now be a part of the NFL's health plan for life. This is powerfully important for players who previously were kicked off all plans five years after retirement. Getting private insurance after playing in the NFL is a nightmare, as your body is a spiderweb of preexisting conditions. Retirees will also receive up to a $1 billion increase in benefits, with $620 million going to increasing pensions for those who retired before 1993.

Yes, owners received a bigger piece of the pie. They also preserved the practice of having Roger Goodell maintain absolute power as commissioner. He is both the person who dispenses punishment and the person to whom players have to appeal when suspended. I also agree with Brian Frederick, director of the Sports Fans Coalition (SFC), who commented that it's a problem that "fans were forced to sit on the sidelines during these negotiations, despite the massive public subsidies and antitrust exemptions we grant the league."[15] This is especially true given that, as SFC reported, thirty-one of thirty-two NFL stadiums have received direct public subsidies, ten of them 100 percent publicly financed and at least nineteen of them 75 percent publicly financed.[16]

But in the end, this deal—against all odds—is a victory for players, their families, their health, and their long-term financial solvency. It's also proof for workers across the country that there is power in labor and there is power in solidarity.

Unfortunately, a different consensus emerged in the sports media: like coaches of six-year-old kids getting trophies after soccer practice, they declared everyone a winner. *Sports Illustrated's* Peter King believed that Goodell and Smith should be co-winners of the magazine's Sportsperson of the Year award, as his colleague Don Banks trilled that the golden goose would lay eggs another day: "Neither side got everything they wanted, but good negotiations are like that. Now that this CBA fight is almost over, and labor peace seems finally at hand, both the players and the owners have the right to claim success."[17]

These parroted assessments missed the true, overarching story of the longest work stoppage in NFL history. At the opening kickoff, the sides weren't even close to evenly matched. The NFL's owners had a promise from their television partners of four billion dollars in "lockout insurance" even if the games didn't air. They had a workforce with a career shelf life of three to four years, understandably skittish about missing a single paycheck. And most critically, ownership had what they thought was the overwhelming support of public opinion—after all, in past labor disputes, fans sided against those who "get paid to play a game." What the NFLPA did was the equivalent of the team from *Friday Night Lights* squeaking out a victory against the 1986 Chicago Bears. It was really workers, in an age of austerity, beating back the bosses and showing that solidarity is the only way to win.

What the NBA Didn't Do

Just as the NFL negotiations ended, the national Occupy movement took off. At that point, the NFLPA had a ten-year CBA in hand and a season to play. But for the NBA, whose lockout was continuing deep into the fall, there was a clear opportunity to connect with this emerging struggle. After all, a movement directly confronting the 1 percent should have resonated with both players and the National Basketball Players Association.

If you really want to talk about corporate greed pile-driving the interests of "the 99 percent," look no further than the NBA. The league's billionaire owners locked their doors and threatened to cancel the 2011–12 season following the most lucrative year in league history. They locked out not only the players' union but thousands of low-wage workers—the people cleaning the arenas, parking the cars, and selling the overpriced, foamy swill the league calls beer. It's the 1 percent version of the high pick-and-roll, their go-to play: magically spinning our tax dollars into their profits. While workers are laid off and the infrastructure of our cities rots, economist David Berri has noted that $2 billion has gone into building eight new NBA facilities. Of that amount, $1.75 billion has come out of our pockets. That number doesn't include the $2 billion in tax dollars being funneled into the Atlantic Yards project for the new Brooklyn Nets. For NBA commissioner David Stern to leave public subsidies out of his math and claim that twenty-two of thirty NBA owners were "losing money" demonstrated his utter contempt for the taxpayers keeping his league afloat.[18]

But the NBA players—even as they were engaging in bitter, nasty, round-the-clock negotiations a ten-minute cab ride from Zuccotti Park—didn't take any steps to forge ties with Occupy. There was one exception: NBA player and union executive board member Etan Thomas, who spent time in the park and found himself "energized and inspired." He then wrote for ESPN.com,

> While the issues raised by the Wall Street occupiers differ from the issues of this lockout, aren't there obvious parallels in power imbalance? Who is in the same position of power as the 1 percent? Who wants a bailout for their own mismanagement decisions? Who is more closely aligned with the corporate interests from which the Wall Street occupiers are looking to reclaim the country? [19]

These were important questions that could have set the stage for a sincere fight with NBA owners for league control. Unfortunately, a different tack was taken. In the end, the bitter adversaries, NBA commissioner David Stern and National Basketball Players Association executive director Billy Hunter, emerged smiling ear to ear, discarding their suit jackets for bunchy, seasonal sweaters from the Heathcliff Huxtable collection. Only then-NBPA president and then–L.A. Lakers co-captain Derek Fisher kept his suit, and a very dour game face. (The look on his face probably augured his bitter 2012 separation from Hunter and the union.)

Truth be told, Fisher looked like he'd just emerged from a Turkish prison—and his expression fit the moment. Forget the cuddly sweaters. Ignore the fact that the basketball-player-in-chief President Obama gave the deal a "thumbs-up." Disregard the avalanche of tweets from your favorite star players about how excited they were to get back to work. Once you wipe away the confetti, what NBA players settled for was a massive transfer of wealth from players to owners: $3 billion over the next decade, extracted from those we pay to see and given to those who have spent the last twenty years raising ticket prices, taking public money for arenas, and treating fans and taxpayers like the cowering, abused partners we are. Owners locked the doors, and now players have less money, fewer benefits, and less security.

The deal will also do more to help big-market teams that spend carelessly than the much-discussed poor, small-market squads. In other words, nothing in this collective bargaining agreement changes the basic contours for reaching a championship. And there are no promises that the owners will plow their newfound lucre into their teams. There are no assurances that any funds will be earmarked for coaches or scouts, nor that any of these savings will translate into lower ticket prices or NBA package discounts for fans. All it means is that the owners have received a financial windfall because, simply, they own and we don't. Now Donald Sterling, proud owner of the L.A. Clippers as well as an archipelago of low-income housing, can buy some more slums. Now Phil Anschutz, minority boss of the Lakers, can keep funding conservative boutique magazines and underwrite the fight against the teaching of evolution in schools. Now Clay Bennett and Aubrey McClendon of the Oklahoma City Thunder can propel more anti-gay legislation onto election-year ballots. Now Dick DeVos of the Orlando Magic can give even more generously to Focus on the Family.

The deal and its historic cuts should have stung every player in the league. Scoop Jackson of ESPN made the case about why there was something greater at stake than just money, linking it to the Occupy movements:

This here is taking place in front of our very eyes, in our lifetime. Occupying our lives: Wall Street. . . . Because this

lockout is no longer about basketball. Any of us who still believe it is are either dense, dim or dumb. Or all three . . . For
the players, this is a "stand for something or fall for anything"
moment. . . . A moment that many, many years from now will
allow them to say, "At least we were once about something
more than just basketball."[20]

In the end, however, it was approved overwhelmingly by the
players, and for understandable reasons. When your average career
is only six years, giving up one-sixth of your professional earning
potential doesn't feel like an option. As a result, their contracts are
now weakened, even though they *are* the game. For the millions
who paid good money to watch Chicago Bulls player Michael Jordan soar, no one ever paid a cent to see Charlotte Hornets owner
Michael Jordan sit and sulk in a suit. Athletes are different than
typical workers, and not just because their paychecks tower over
our own. They are different because they fulfill a dual role in pro-
duction as both workers and product. They are the shoemaker and
the shoe. Or as former Washington football great Brian Mitchell
said to me, "In a restaurant, a chef cooks a steak. In sports, we are
the chef and we are the steak."

It didn't have to be this way. The players let David Stern's PR
machine define them as greedy millionaires, insensitive to the public's suffering in these hard economic times. There were no players
with concussions to point to, no unguaranteed contracts, no grave-
yard of middle-aged men who wouldn't see their fiftieth birthday.
In other words, it just wasn't football. But there was still potential,
as Etan Thomas demonstrated, to connect and amplify the issues
by bringing grievances out of the boardroom and into the public
sphere. They didn't, and they paid the price. Given how little labor
issues make it into the mainstream press, we all paid a price as well
by not seeing this struggle amplified.

What Could Have Been

The most prominent athlete to speak at Occupy Wall Street turned out to be someone from 1968, the aforementioned Dr. John Carlos. When Dr. Carlos arrived at Zuccotti Park, with me trailing behind him, he saw a sea of ordered chaos. People of all backgrounds and ages were packed shoulder to shoulder. Police stood at attention, glowering down from their majestic horses. Homemade signs ranging from "Undocumented immigrants are part of the 99%" to "We Remember Troy Davis" to "Tax the Rich!" encircled the square. John Carlos looked at me and said, "It's great to be home."

With the help of the Occupy Wall Street regulars who invited us to speak, we worked our way to the front of the general assembly. When I asked the head of the facilitation team if John Carlos could say just a few words, she looked at me quizzically and asked who he was. I answered by doing a poor man's impression of the medal-stand moment, bowing my head and raising my fist. Her face lit up. This was someone born years, possibly decades, after 1968 and she got it. John Carlos was able to get on the "People's Mic." "I am here for you," he said in his raspy voice. "Why? Because I am you. We're here forty-three years later because there's a fight still to be won. This day is not for us but for our children to come."

The next day, we were on a cable network television program and Dr. Carlos was asked, "Do you really see a connection between what you did at the Olympics and what these 'young people' are doing sleeping outside in Zuccotti Park?" Dr. Carlos responded, "Oh, I absolutely see a connection. The connection is very clear. In 1968, given the injustices in the world, there was no more appropriate place to stand up than at the Olympic Games. In 2011, given the economic injustices in the world, there is no more appropriate place to stand up than right there on Wall Street."

Carlos and I did multiple teach-ins at Occupy encampments

and my experience was that far from any hostility toward athletes or their salaries, there was instead a great eagerness to connect the movement to all aspects of life. If NBA players had seized this chance to connect, it would have been as daring and principled as Scoop Jackson suggested.

Occupy the Super Bowl

If athlete response to the Occupy movements was anemic in the heat of struggle, fans didn't wait for them to take the lead. This past year, activists in Indiana's labor and Occupy movements took the people's microphone to the apex of corporate sports branding itself: the Super Bowl. The Republican-led statehouse was about to pass legislation that would make Indiana a "right to work" state. For those uninitiated in Orwellian doublespeak, the term "right to work" is a phrase of grotesque sophistry; it entails smashing unions and making it harder for nonunion workplaces to get basic job protections. This drew peals of protest throughout the state, with the Occupy and labor movements front-and-center from small towns to Governor Mitch Daniels's door at the statehouse.

Whether out of simple arrogance or sheer idiocy, Daniels and friends timed this legislation with Indianapolis's hosting the 2012 Super Bowl. The Super Bowl is perennially the Woodstock for the 1 percent, a Romney-esque cavalcade of private planes and private parties. But this year, over one hundred and fifty people marched through the pre–Super Bowl street fair in downtown Indianapolis with signs that read "Occupy the Super Bowl," "Fight the Lie," and "Workers United Will Prevail." Occupy the Super Bowl also became a T-shirt, featured on the NBC Sports website.

The protests shed light on the reality of life for working families in Indianapolis. Unemployment at the time of the big game was at 13.3 percent, and 21 percent for African American families; two of every five African American families with a child under five were living below the poverty line. Such pain amid the gloss of the Super Bowl and the looming right-to-work legislation was, for many, a catalyst to get into the streets.

April Burke, a former schoolteacher and member of a local Occupy chapter, said to me, "I see right-to-work for what it is: an attack on not only organized labor but on all working-class people. . . . Rushing the passage of RTW in the state of Indiana on the eve of the Super Bowl is an insult to the thousands of union members who built Lucas [Oil] Stadium as well as the members of the National Football League Players Association who issued a statement condemning the RTW bill."

Bloomberg, which no one will mistake for the *New Masses,* headlined an article "Super Bowl Lands on Taxpayers' Backs as Indianapolis Stadium Deal Sours." Bloomberg described a state of affairs in Indy where "Super Bowl fans are riding zip lines through downtown" while "taxpayers are digging deeper in their pockets to pay for the stadium where the game will be played." They reported that local officials had had to hike sales and hospitality taxes to pay off $43 million in "unexpected financing costs." No amount of extra shifts for waiters and parking lot attendants could match the tax burden those same individuals would endure in order to play host. But at least city planners can have that zip line and the "800,000-square-foot exposition" called "the NFL Experience."[21]

The state's union leaders pulled back from any kind of public showing in front of the stadium or on the Super Bowl grounds. Nancy Guyott, president of the Indiana AFL-CIO, said, "While we understand the anger and frustration of working Hoosiers' [*sic*] over the disgraceful passage of the so-called, 'right to work' bill, the appropriate outlet will be at the ballot box, not the Super Bowl."[22] Similarly, DeMaurice Smith said that the NFLPA was committed to challenging other states where right-to-work laws have been proposed and showed up in Indianapolis to protest before the big game but remained ambiguous about game-day protests.

Given the politics that already swamp the Super Bowl—from corporate branding to military commercialism to regionally run antiabortion ads—why should labor be at all sheepish about having a voice on game day?

Luckily, the union leadership's words were not law that Sunday. If the Occupy movement has taught people anything, it's that fortune favors the bold. The *Wall Street Journal* quoted Tim Janko, a steelworker from northwest Indiana, and Perry Stabler, a retired steelworker, who both said they would be seen and heard on game day. "I'm going to picket the Super Bowl because this is wrong," Janko said. "I'm going to have a Teamster drive me into town." Stabler also commented, "Union workers built that stadium, they should have the right to demonstrate in front of it."

The people of Indiana were angry, and it showed. They came from Indianapolis, Bloomington, Anderson, and beyond. All of these proud trade unionists and Occupy activists showed up even though the AFL-CIO explicitly instructed them not to protest on the day of the big game. That's why it's so important that the people were a presence, leaving energized and excited about forging connections between the Occupy and the labor movements. After all, we don't have $3 million for a thirty-second ad—we just have the ability to gather and raise our collective voice.

This is at the heart of the Occupy movement: the claiming of space so grievances can be heard. From Zuccotti Park to Lucas Oil Stadium, people gathered to just say, "Enough." That sports has been both an inspiration and a target of this movement is remarkable enough—and the link between them bore far more dramatic consequences in the struggles for justice, democracy, and freedom in the Middle East.

· 2 ·

"You Have to Be an Ultra from Within": Soccer and the Arab Spring

They are known around the world by several distinguishing characteristics. They are young. They are clandestine. They reject politics. And they live to cheer and fight, though not necessarily in that order. They are the ultras, hyperintense soccer fan clubs that show allegiance to their teams with colors, fireworks, and pitched street fights with their opponents' fans or, on a particularly "fun" night, the police. Even though they exist across Europe, the Middle East, and North Africa, they are bound by a common phrase: ACAB (all cops are bastards). In many countries with an authoritarian bent, the clubs are allowed to exist and even thrive, under the tacit understanding that it's better for young, frustrated men to take out their anger on themselves and the police than on the government.

But what happens to the ultras when real revolution breaks out? Does their hatred of politics relegate them to the sideline or do they use their organization, fighting skills, and anger to aid the struggle? What makes this question particularly potent is a long-standing debate in the history of sports over the question of "bread and circuses"—whether being a sports fan represents a withdrawal from, or even the very negation of, political consciousness. Is it possible that upheaval in the streets could change, on a dime, the ways in which we perceive ourselves as fans?

We have seen all of this play out in real time in Egypt. Since 2007 the ultras have been Egypt's one consistent nexus for expressive anger and practical experience in the ancient art of street fighting. For years these clubs operated as a social safety valve, channeling the anger of young, often poor men. As Rabab el-Mahdi, an assistant professor of political science at the American University in Cairo, said, "Since the Ultras were created, they were always targeted by state security. They are seen as a mob or as hooligans, so they developed skills that none of the middle class was forced to develop. Plus they come from backgrounds where such skills are needed on daily basis just as survival mechanisms."[1]

Most of the ultras' fighting over the years was directed at other clubs—exemplified by the rivalry between the fan organizations of teams al-Ahly and Zamalek—rather than the government. The clubs had also long been allowed by the country's president for life Hosni Mubarak's security forces to set up "pyro," or flares, during and after soccer matches; most famously, they safely self-organized the lighting of three hundred simultaneous flares. Over the years, the ultras were essentially allowed to train themselves as effective street revolutionaries—as long as their actions were bled of any political content.

This was only sustainable for so long, however, especially because the ultras were treated like punching bags by the police. "If you went to a stadium and saw how some policeman riding a horse could lash ultras members with a whip for no apparent reason," said Ahmed Gaafar, a founder of the Ultras White Knights (UWK), the fan group of Zamalek SC, "you would understand the nature of the relationship between the police and ultras groups."[2]

Egypt's rebellion finally burst into open view on January 25,

2011. With each foray into the streets, the gatherings in Cairo's Tahrir Square became more militant and more unified. It was thought that Mubarak could ride out the unrest until February 9 and 10, when Egyptian workers went on strike. By February 11, the military had made it clear to Mubarak that it was time to go. In eighteen days, the dictator was facing criminal charges.

During the first week of the revolution, when the direction of the struggle looked most precarious, the most organized, militant fan clubs, Ultras Ahlawy and Ultras White Knights, put their years of experience to vital use. They set up checkpoints. They secured neighborhoods. They built barricades. They kept the state police at bay. As one Egyptian revolutionary said to me, "In those first days, the ultras were indispensable. But the hardest thing, it felt like at times, was to keep them all focused on the goal [of removing Mubarak] and keep them from killing each other."

Distinguished by their uniform of skinny jeans and hoodies, they quickly became seen as heroes in Tahrir Square, described as "those courageous guys." "They stayed there in the square almost through 100 hours of fighting," protester Mosa'ab Elshamy said. "It's easy to notice them because of their use of Molotov cocktails, their extreme courage and recklessness, their chants. They became a common sight."[3]

The ultras' chant that Elshamy referenced was:

Regime! Be very scared of us!
We are coming tonight with intent
The supporters of Al Ahly/Zamalek will fire everything up
God almighty will make us victorious!
Go, hooligans![4]

Mubarak responded by ordering the Egyptian Football Association (EFA) to suspend all league games, thinking that would keep the clubs from congregating. But that just created more idle time for the ultras and more chances for them to interact with each other. When this looked like a failed strategy, the police attacked people wearing their soccer colors in public and forcibly entered the homes of club leaders in the middle of the night to beat them in their sleep. As one ultra named Assad said to CNN, "The more they tried to put pressure on us, the more we grew in cult status. The Ministry and the media, they would call us a gang, as violent. It wasn't just supporting a team; you were fighting a system and the country as a whole. We were fighting the police, fighting the government, fighting for our rights . . . this was something new."[5]

Instead of fighting each other, the clubs started organizing committees to continue securing neighborhoods and barricading city squares. In an interview with al-Jazeera, Alaa Abd el-Fattah, a prominent Egyptian blogger, said, "The ultras have played a more significant role than any political group on the ground at this moment." He then joked, "Maybe we should get the ultras to rule the country."[6]

Not even many local Egyptians foresaw this. In 2010, the dominant view was best expressed by Egyptian journalist Adel Iskandar, who said, "Fundamentally, the sport is the polar opposite of politics [in Egypt]." But in fact, the involvement of the clubs signaled more than just the intervention of sports fans. The ultras' entry into the political struggle also meant the entry of the poor, the disenfranchised, and the masses of young people in Egypt for whom soccer was the only outlet. As James Dorsey, who writes the indispensable blog The Turbulent World of Middle East Soccer, noted, "The involvement of organized soccer fans in Egypt's anti-government protests constitutes every Arab government's worst nightmare. Soccer, alongside Islam, offers a rare platform in the Middle East, a region populated by authoritarian regimes that control all public spaces, for the venting of pent-up anger and frustration."[7]

Dorsey's statement proved prophetic when it was announced that Muammar Gadhafi had ordered the Libyan Football Federation to ban soccer matches for the foreseeable future. According to government sources, Gadhafi feared that soccer could be the vessel for delivering Egypt's revolutionary fervor to Libya's doorstep.

The critical role of Egypt's soccer clubs in the recent revolution may surprise us, but the history of soccer in the region gave clues that this could happen. When the pre-ultras Egyptian soccer clubs were founded more than a century ago, cheering in the stadium and antigovernment organizing walked together in comfort. Egypt's most prominent team, al-Ahly, started its club in 1907 as a place to organize national resistance against British colonial rule. Translated into English, the club's name means "the National," to mark its unapologetically political stance against European colonialism. Al-Ahly likes to boast that it's been the team with the most political and most working-class fans. It's also a team whose players have felt comfortable making incendiary political statements on the pitch, in direct violation of FIFA dictates. It's no coincidence that it was al-Ahly's star player Mohamed Aboutrika, a.k.a. "the Smiling Assassin," who in 2008 famously raised his jersey to reveal a T-shirt that read "Sympathize with Gaza." During the Egyptian Revolution, Aboutrika regularly joined prayers in Tahrir Square.[8]

In 2007, inspired by Italy's apolitical, rowdy, and often violent soccer clubs, the ultras formed as a place where Egyptians expressed their alienation from Egypt's then-dreary political world. "Soccer is bigger than politics. It's about escapism. The average Ahly fan is a guy who lives in a one bedroom flat with his wife, mother-in-law and five kids. He is paid minimum wage and his life sucks. The only good thing about his life is that for two hours on a Friday, he goes to the stadium and watches Ahly," said a leader of al-Ahly's ultras.[9]

When the revolution began, this changed dramatically. As Assad said, laughing, "I don't want to say we were solely responsible for bringing down Mubarak! Our role was to make people dream, letting them know if a cop hits you, you can hit them back. This was a police state. Our role started earlier than the revolution."[10]

The al-Ahly ultras were not the only Egyptian soccer club to take to the streets. The Zamalek ultras, known as the Ultras White Knights, also jumped into the fray. Zamalek is one of the most popular and successful soccer teams in the entire Arab world. It started in 1911 as the club that would accept players from all ethnic, religious, and socioeconomic backgrounds—which was remarkable in an era when American baseball excluded people of color and country clubs shut their doors to blacks, Jews, and even Catholics. After Egypt's 1919 revolution, the club was renamed after King Farouk, but following the coup against the king in 1952, it was known forevermore as Zamalek and continued its historic rivalry with al-Ahly. These differences in history are reflected in the teams' colors: al-Ahly wears the red of the precolonial Egyptian flag, while Zamalek wears the white of the British imperial class and the deposed Farouk.

Decades of rivalry washed away during the revolution. As Mohammed of the Ultras White Knights said, "On the Day of Rage [January 28], we made a plan. . . . On our own, it was nothing. But together as a group in the square we were a big power. . . . 10,000–15,000 people fighting without any fear. The ultras were the leaders of the battle." Ahmed Ezzat, the general coordinator of the Popular Committees for Protecting the Revolution, said to Ahram Online, "All demonstrators always welcome the Ultras members in Tahrir Square. They are highly organized and are not looking for any media attention. They have the tendency to struggle in hard times; they are perceived to be comrades in the project of the revolution and have robustly supported the revolutionaries all along."[11]

As Ashraf el-Sherif, a professor at the American University in Cairo, wrote in *Egypt Independent,*

> When the 25 January revolution erupted, observers discovered that the only organized group in Egypt with the combative experience to deal with Central Security Forces and the Ministry of Interior was the ultras, not the Muslim Brotherhood, the April 6 Youth Movement or the National Assembly for Change. They had mastered attack and defense strategies that helped reduce losses. They knew how to sustain active resistance.[12]

Ultras even expressed frustration with their own beloved players, many of whom did not participate in the struggle. In March, al-Ahly Ultras unfolded a huge banner addressed to players during their team's contest against Harras el-Hodood that read: "We followed you everywhere but in the hard times we didn't find you." While most of the established soccer players stayed away from Tahrir, that wasn't the case across the board. Nader el-Sayed, former goalkeeper of Egypt's national team, joined the protesters after the fall of Mubarak woke him up. He said, "It was something I had waited for so, so long." Now el-Sayed is politically active with the moderate al-Wasat Islamist party, in addition to running a soccer academy. "We had a popular revolution, now it's time for the political revolution. I wanted to join a political party, not a religious movement," added Sayed, in criticism of the Muslim Brotherhood. "We need to participate without using intellectual, religious or economic terrorism."[13]

Today in Egypt the ultras form the heart of a rich mosaic of resistance, a remarkable example of the capacity of sports to bring people together. The great author of *Soccer in Sun and Shadow,*

Eduardo Galeano, in a different time and context, once wrote, "The dictatorship of fear is over." Truer words about Egypt could never be spoken. As Assad said, "The police would abuse us every day. Now it's our time."[14]

But the military and conservative Islamist parties have learned lessons, as well. The military suspended all soccer matches that were to be played around January 25, 2012, the anniversary of the revolution, in order to avoid clashes with the ultras. As James Dorsey wrote, "The postponement of the soccer matches reflects the government and the EFA's concern that the soccer fan and youth groups will use the January 25 celebrations to press their demand for the immediate return of the military to its barracks—a demand that is strengthened by the fact that the country now has an elected parliament."[15]

The postrevolution Muslim Brotherhood has attempted to marginalize the ultras by developing a "pro-sports" position, unlike the more traditional Islamist parties. "We support sports in general and encourage them. Sports flourished in the age of Islam, so why shouldn't they under the Islamists? We are looking to encourage more sporting activities nationwide. . . . Islam doesn't have any problem with soccer and other sports," said Brotherhood spokesman Mahmoud Ghozlan to the newspaper *al-Akhbar el-Yom*. This position seemed to be working until impatience with the military's chosen pace of change combined with the worst "soccer riot" in the country's history.[16]

Port Said

In the year following the fall of Mubarak and the subsequent ascension of the military, there has been a concerted effort to get the country out of the streets and back to pursuits of work and play. But there is no turning back in Egypt. If there was a moment that showed just how much has changed, it was the massacre at Port Said.

On February 1, 2012. A soccer game became a killing field, with at least seventy-four spectators dead and as many as a thousand injured. After the visiting al-Ahly team lost to al-Masri in a 3–1 upset victory, al-Masri fans rushed the field and attacked the al-Ahly cheering section. There were stabbings and beatings, but the majority of deaths resulted from asphyxiation as many fans, including Ultras Ahlawy members, were crushed against locked stadium doors. Port Said survivors describe a situation where exits were blocked by military police; stadium lights were turned off, adding to the sense of panic; and hundreds of riot police watched on in silence, as if under orders to just sit back and do nothing.

Mohamed Aboutrika, the aforementioned beloved al-Ahly star, immediately announced his retirement in the aftermath. A distraught Aboutrika said, "This is not football. This is a war and people are dying in front of us. . . . This is a horrible situation, and today can never be forgotten."[17]

The Western media immediately used the tragedy to call for a crackdown on the ultras. The *New York Times* wrote, "The deadliest soccer riot anywhere in more than 15 years, it also illuminated the potential for savagery among the organized groups of die-hard fans known here as ultras who have added a volatile element to the street protests since Mr. Mubarak's exit."[18] Other Western observers sympathetic to the revolution feared, with good cause, that the riots would strengthen the military dictatorship, which was slow to hand over power to civilian rule.

The Port Said carnage, however, birthed profoundly unexpected results. Instead of provoking concern about "lawlessness" in post-revolutionary Egypt, the anger and sadness had the effect of reviving the revolution.

On the ground, a new reality quickly took shape, fueled by a widespread belief that the military, either through benign neglect or malignant intent, let the killings happen. No sector of society has been silent. Abbas Mekhimar, head of the parliament's defense committee, said, "This is a complete crime. This is part of the scenario of fueling chaos against Egypt." Dee Salas, of the Egyptian Football Association, noted, "The government is getting back at the ultras. They are saying: 'You protest against us, you want democracy and freedom. Here is a taste of your democracy and freedom.'"[19]

Even the Muslim Brotherhood, which has made constant efforts to marginalize the ultras, issued a statement saying, "The lack of security in the Port Said stadium confirms that there is invisible planning that is behind this unjustified massacre. The authorities have been negligent. We fear that some officers are punishing the people for their revolution."[20]

The Revolutionary Socialists, an Egyptian organization with a grassroots following in the streets, said, "The clumsily-hatched plot, which could not conceal the shameless complicity of the police . . . carries only one message to the revolutionaries: the revolution must continue and achieve its goals."[21]

As the Revolutionary Socialists make clear, the widespread support for the ultras stems from the role they played in the toppling of Mubarak. One Egyptian blogger testified personally to their heroism, writing,

> The ultras maybe not be saints, but . . . I probably owe life and limb to the ultras who defended me and other protesters during the toughest days of the revolution. The ultras were always the calvary [sic] during protests. . . . The ultras may not be philosophical or articulate, and they do not have political agenda, but they fully believed in the just cause of the revolution.[22]

It is also clear that the al-Ahly ultras have now become a leading target of the military. They wear that target proudly, chanting at games (and I'm told this rhymes in Arabic),

Oh you MPs
You turned out to be more rotten than the Police
Raise the prison walls higher and higher
Tomorrow the revolution will lay them to waste
Oh brother, write on the cell wall
Junta rule is shameful and treasonous
Down Down with Junta rule! [23]

Not only are the people coming to the defense of the ultras; remarkably, ultras from opposing clubs have pledged to join forces, understanding the attack on Ahlawy as an attack on all of them. After Port Said, the Ahlawy ultras themselves released a statement against not al-Masri but the military, saying, "They want to punish us and execute us for our participation in the revolution against suppression." They then vowed a "new war in defense of the revolution." [24]

These proved to be more than just words. The following Thursday, after a blasé statement by military chief Field Marshal Tantawi, protests exploded in Cairo, Suez, and Port Said itself. The clashes took place on the anniversary of the Battle of the Camels, when Mubarak sent armed thugs riding into Tahrir Square on camels and ultras were credited with bravely standing in their path.

In Cairo, at least ten thousand protesters marched to the Interior Ministry building near Tahrir Square. According to Health Ministry official Adel Adawi, the battle that followed resulted in 388 protesters being injured. The flags unfurled side by side were of traditional rivals, al-Ahly and Zamalek. The chants were, "We dreamed of change. They fooled us and brought us a field marshal instead."

In Suez, thousands took to the streets, braving repeated tear gas shelling. But most significant were the thousands of al-Masri fans who gathered in Port Said, demanding answers from police.

This reemergence of the ultra clubs as a united force against the military regime should send shivers down the backs of the comfortable in Cairo. Last year, as one Egyptian activist said to me, "Getting the ultras to work together in Tahrir might have been the toughest part about deposing Mubarak. They really hate each other. They would spit when saying the other club's name." But after Port Said, an injury to one group of ultras was seen as an injury to all. As James Dorsey wrote, the aftermath of Port Said has sparked "a reconciliation among once implacable foes while at the same time solidifying emerging fault lines in Egyptian society."[25] Throughout the past year, the ultras have fought together at antimilitary protests, in opposition to the Egyptian Football Association, and against the presence of the Israeli embassy. (We should remember that the Israeli government opposed and decried the deposing of Mubarak.) They bled and died together, even as they became more politically isolated by the military's promise of an orderly transfer of power.

Following the Port Said carnage, the ultras have created their own revolutionary challenge to the military council. Despite continuous efforts to marginalize the ultras, they are now at the center of the stage of history. With them, the Egyptian Revolution returns to the Egyptian streets.

But while Egypt's is a story of sports and politics coming together to fight for a better day, the situation in Bahrain showed the price of losing, for the masses and any athlete who might join them.

Bahrain

The Arab Spring reverberated powerfully in the sprawling kingdom of Bahrain among its 1.2 million citizens. On February 14, the same day as the first demonstrations in Madison, Wisconsin, hundreds of thousands of people poured into the Bahraini streets demanding democracy and economic justice. On the eighteenth, five protesters were killed, with more deaths to come. But that only caused the demonstrations to swell. That March, the country's royal family eventually called upon the Saudi army to help them quash the revolt, which they did with great enthusiasm. The final death toll isn't known, but we do know that dozens of unarmed protesters were shot and killed. President Barack Obama and the U.S. government said precious little about any of this. This isn't just oversight or happenstance. Bahrain happily hosts the U.S. Navy's Fifth Fleet and has pledged to do so for another fifty years. It appears that this favor has given them carte blanche to spill the blood of peaceful protesters.

This wasn't the first revolt in Bahrain's history, but it was by far the most serious. The country is run by the al-Khalifas—a royal family so decayed with gluttony, excess, and corruption that they could be honorary Trumps. Once the wave started across the region, Bahrain was ripe for rebellion against autocracy. Chris Toensing, the editor of the *Middle East Report,* said to me,

> Because it is located atop the hydrocarbon jackpot of the world in the Persian Gulf, Bahrain has the image of a wealthy nation. In fact a large part of the native population is poor. That poverty plus the sectarianism chauvinism and tyranny of the royal family have made the country restive for decades. The 2011 revolt is but the largest and most brutally repressed of a series of popular struggles for justice.

Among the protesters was a superstar athlete by the name of A'ala Hubail. Hubail is a legend in the world of Bahraini soccer. In 2004, along with his brother Mohamed, the twenty-eight-year-old national team captain led his upstart squad on a rollicking run to the Asian Cup semifinals. Hubail was able to control the pace of the entire pitch in a masterful performance and then became the first Bahraini player to win the prestigious Golden Boot award after scoring five goals against the continent's best teams. After winning this honor, A'ala became known in the press as "the Golden Boy." But it turns out he was golden only as long as he shut his mouth, scored pretty goals, and just played ball.

The Hubail brothers, unlike many athletes, could not remain on the sidelines. In addition to being a soccer star, A'ala is a certified paramedic and EMT, and both brothers decided to go to the demonstrations to help wounded protesters. A'ala was also seen daring to chant, "Sunnis and Shias are brothers."

The Hubails were soon informed that, at the behest of the Bahraini royal family, they had been expelled from the national squad. Both brothers, along with two other players, were then handcuffed and frog-marched off the practice field in front of shocked teammates. They were then taken into custody "on an indefinite basis." The day before their sacking and arrest, a popular Bahraini state television interview program had grilled A'ala Hubail for showing up to the demonstrations. They had shown footage of both brothers caught on camera in what the broadcasters proudly called an effort to "shame the sports stars." Describing the demonstrators as "violent protesters" and "stray hyenas," the state news report failed to mention that Hubail acted as a volunteer nurse at the protest. Hubail should have been lauded as a true hero; instead, his efforts were branded an open act of aggression against the state.[26]

The following day, the brothers were imprisoned and isolated from each other. Their heads were shaved, and then they were tortured. Teammate Ali Saeed and Anwar al-Makki, Bahrain's internationally ranked table-tennis champion, were also tortured.

"They put me in the room for beatings," said Mohamed Hubail. "One of the people who hit me said: 'I'm going to break your legs.'

They knew who we were. There was a special room for the torture." Hubail's words are echoed in ESPN interviews with al-Makki and sports journalist Faisal Hayyat.

"They would bring an electric cable, blindfold the person and put them on the floor," Mr. Makki said.

"I was blindfolded. I couldn't see what was happening. He put a cable in my hand and said: 'Now I'll turn the electricity on,'" Mr. Hayyat added.

Mohamed was beaten on the bottoms of his feet.

When they were released, A'ala told ESPN, "We were living in a nightmare of fear and horror. . . . I served my country with love and will continue as much as I can. But I won't forget the experience, which I went through for all my life. What happened to me was a cost of fame. Participating in the athletes' rally was not a crime."[27]

Friends and relatives said the men had been threatened with further abuse if they spoke out but gave details of what they knew of the men's treatment in jail. "The first two weeks after they were arrested were the worst. They were beaten all the time. They still have marks on their bodies," said one close relative who did not want to be named. "But the men who were beating them were not Bahraini. They didn't care who they were," said a friend of the players.[28]

Mohamed told the Associated Press that he was still reckoning with his experience and is not set on returning to any Bahraini team. "Sure, I want to play. But first we need a solution to all of this," he said. "I need to know what is going to happen to me. For our community, the nation, how long are we going to be like this?"[29]

The Hubail brothers were just the most prominent athletes affected in what has become an ugly crackdown on the country's Jocks for Justice. Another national soccer team player, defender Sayed Mohamed Adnan, fled to Australia, where he joined a team called the Brisbane Roar after having endured three months of prison beatings and torture.

Bahrain's royal family announced after the initial flurry of massacres and arrests that two hundred athletes had been indefinitely suspended on charges of "supporting the popular revolution in the country." Among them were nationally known basketball, volleyball, and handball players. The AP quoted a government official, speaking under the cloak of anonymity, as saying that these athletes had been branded "against the government" for having supported "anti-government" protests. No other specifics were given. All two hundred had also been banned from international play—and all two hundred, like the overwhelming majority of demonstrators, were part of the country's oppressed Shia Muslim majority.[30]

Some athletes suffered an even worse fate. Bahrain national soccer team goalkeeper Ali Saeed, champion bodybuilder Tareq al-Fursani, and national basketball team player Hassan al-Dirazi were sentenced to a year in prison for participating in the protests. Shamefully, yet completely unsurprisingly, all of these punishments, including those levied against the Hubail brothers, were backed by the Bahrain Football Association. They explained this by saying, "The suspension falls under misconduct, and the breaching of the rules and regulations of sporting clubs . . . not to engage in political affairs."[31]

A'ala Hubail has largely remained silent—but did ask, in one interview, why the world has chosen to do the same. He also hopes that his suffering will result in more than just fear. As a link in the chain of events from the Middle East to the American Midwest, Hubail was without a doubt thrown into something much larger than he must have thought at the start. Above all, he proved that the stakes for all sports people, athletes and fans alike, have never been higher.

·3·

Today's World Cup and
Olympics: *Invictus* in Reverse

I n Chile, they called it El Ladrillo: the Brick. Drafted by "the
Chicago Boys"—disciples of University of Chicago neoliberal
economics professor Milton Friedman—the many-thousand-page
economic manifesto was printed on an infamous day in Chile's history, September 11, 1973. On that "other 9/11," Chile's presidential
palace was bombed, "Compañero Presidente" Salvador Allende was
murdered, dissidents were rounded up for torture and execution,
and General Augusto Pinochet seized power. The Brick then became Pinochet's economic compass. It guided the country through
"the Miracle of Chile": two decades of slash-and-burn privatiza-
tion, deregulation, and engineered inequality, all in the name of
"development."

Today Pinochet is reviled and gone, but the Brick has become
a default manifesto for much of the globe. Its most ardent sponsors now coincidentally bear its name as an acronym: BRIC (Brazil,
Russia, India, and China). These ambitious nations are attempting
to establish themselves as the future of the global economy.

Increasingly, these rising economic powers are also vying for the honor and prestige of hosting international sporting events. In the twenty-first century, such events require more than merely stadiums and hotels. The host country must provide a massive security apparatus, the means to crush any opposition, and the ability to create the kind of "infrastructure" that modern games demand. That means not just stadiums, but sparkling new stadiums; not just security, but the latest in antiterrorist technology; not just new transportation to and from venues, but the removal of unsightly poverty along those paths. That means a willingness to spend billions of dollars in the name of creating a playground for international tourists and multinational sponsors. What this all requires is what the decaying Western powers, at this point, cannot provide: massive deficit spending and a state police infrastructure ready to displace, destroy, or disappear anyone who dares stand in their way.

We saw this in Beijing. In preparation for the 2008 Olympics, the Chinese government reduced entire neighborhoods to rubble and forcibly removed more than at least half a million people. Now Brazil has already started following suit. The country will be hosting both the 2014 World Cup and the 2016 Summer Olympics. Every day in the favelas, the so-called slums that surround Brazil's major cities, the preparations for these international athletic festivals vividly recall the ways of the Brick.

We already have troubling reports as well as cell phone videos made by Brazilian citizens of the bulldozing and "cleansing" of many favelas, all in the name of "making Brazil ready for the Games." In Favela do Metrô, adjacent to Rio de Janeiro's legendary Maracanã stadium, hundreds of families find themselves living on rubble with nowhere to go after a merciless round of demolitions by Brazilian authorities. As the *Guardian* reported, "Redbrick shacks have been cracked open by earth-diggers. Streets are covered in a thick carpet of rubble, litter and twisted metal. By night, crack addicts squat in abandoned shacks, filling sitting rooms with empty bottles, filthy mattresses and crack pipes improvised from plastic cups. The stench of human excrement hangs in the air."[1]

One favela resident, Eduardo Freitas, said, "It looks like you are in Iraq or Libya. I don't have any neighbors left. It's a ghost town." Freitas doesn't need a doctorate from the University of Chicago to understand what is happening. "The World Cup is on its way and they want this area. I think it is inhumane," he said. Fittingly, the Rio housing authority has adopted the same mantra heard forty years ago in Chile—that this is all in the name of "development," and that by refurbishing the area, they are offering favela dwellers "dignity."[2]

Maybe something was lost in translation. Or perhaps a bureaucrat's conception of "dignity" is becoming homeless so your neighborhood can serve as a parking lot for wealthy soccer fans. But this is more than just poor planning. By bulldozing homes before giving families the chance to find new housing or be "relocated," the government is in flagrant violation of basic human rights agreements. Amnesty International, the United Nations, and even the International Olympic Committee—fearful of the damage to its "brand"— are raising concerns.

And there is more "dignity" on the way. According to Julio Cesar Condaque, an activist opposing the leveling of the favelas, "between now and the 2014 World Cup, 1.5 million families will be removed from their homes across the whole of Brazil."[3]

Christopher Gaffney, vice president of the Associação Nacional dos Torcedores (National Fans' Association), said to me, "It's like a freefall into a neoliberal paradise. We are living in cities planned by PR firms and brought into existence by an authoritarian state in conjunction with their corporate partners."

It's been a remarkable journey. Pinochet is now a cautionary memory, universally disgraced in death. Yet somehow, the Brick remains, a millstone around the neck of Latin America. Today Brazil is yet another neoliberal Trojan horse, attempting to push through an agenda the populace would despise were it not wrapped in the trappings of sport. Unlike the case in Beijing, though, we can expect a series of protests in Rio as the games approach. Favela residents have increasingly taken to social media to report on-the-ground accounts of the destruction, and the Brazilian press has been unsparing in its criticism of authorities.[4] Whatever abuses the Brazilian government metes out in the name of the game will not go unnoticed. This time, there are politics on both sides of the pitch. Whether rising grassroots resistance will set a new precedent and help Brazil break away from the continent's darkest political traditions, however, remains to be seen.

Closer on the horizon, London is engulfed in its own set of controversies over "development" and "security." As the most security-conscious, monitored city on the planet prepared for the 2012 Summer Olympic Games—and protesters prepared to demonstrate en masse—it was worth recalling the 2011 street riots that swept across the UK. They were more than just a disturbing sign: they were direct demonstrations of what Olympic priorities can provoke.

Missile Launchers on Apartment Buildings: The 2012 London Games

During London's 2005 bid to secure the 2012 Olympics, the country's ruling Labour Party reached for the Olympic rings with great gusto. In a particularly groveling moment, former prime minister Tony Blair told the IOC, "My promise to you is we will be your very best partners. The entire government are united behind this bid. . . . It is the nation's bid."[5] Was it? London organizer Katie Andrews didn't think so. Instead she expressed both shock and anger: "There was no plebiscite. No vote. Now we have these games being shoved down our throats."[6]

Chief among the Olympic cheerleaders was then–mayor of London Ken Livingstone, who in another life—or an alternative universe—was known as "Red Ken." Livingstone played a major role in whipping up public support for the games. He was quick to point out, in the words of one observer, that "anyone who is against the Olympics is against the investment and infrastructure and jobs which will help the poor."[7]

The Olympics as a social-welfare program sounds lovely until you look closer and realize that it's utterly false. Between cheers, Livingstone also announced that each London council taxpayer would have to shell out £20 a year for twelve years (i.e., £240), even if the games do not make a loss, which is about as likely as seeing the queen wearing leather pants.[8] If there is anything we can count on, it's that Britain's wealthy will make out like bandits, its poor will be squeezed, and Big Ben will end up in the back of a Lausanne pawnshop.

The latest figures have the London games coming in at ten times above the 2005 projected budget, which means the projected taxes will be even higher than Livingstone's rosy calculations. Londoners I spoke with during my own visit to the UK were annoyed at the inconvenience, incensed by the security crackdown—and outraged that there are no tickets available. This is hardly a petty complaint. Corporate partners have gobbled up the seats, leaving the over-whelming majority of the city pressing their noses up against the glass. In London, where pubs dot every block and open onto the streets after work in a party that welcomes all comers (as long as it's not raining), this comprises a cardinal sin. As Neill, one of many bartenders I encountered, said to me, "It's like a big to-do that no one invited us to attend!" The security crackdown and constant paranoia are discomfiting enough. (Fears were even being dissem-inated about possible terrorist attacks from the Irish. Seriously.[9]) But what singes the locals was the idea that the Olympics is a party that will thanklessly stick them with the bill: a hangover from hell without the drunken rapture that by all rights should precede it. The truth is that discontent has long been simmering beneath the surface in London. It just happened to boil over in August 2011. As a week of fiery riots swept the city and beyond, London's Olympic committee was scheduled to stage a beach volleyball exhibition for visiting dignitaries. Representatives from two hundred Olympic committees across the globe descended upon the city just in time for the days of rage. Tory prime minister David Cameron was not amused. Can you imagine the scene? It would be like the Santorum family visiting New York and walking straight into the Gay Pride Parade.

At the very least, the International Olympic Committee now knows what Londoners have known since the day England upset France to win the 2012 games: this multibillion-dollar party rests on the assent of a local populace that's beyond restive. As Tony Travers, a professor at the London School of Economics, said at the time, "There's no doubt that this is a very bad day, a worrying day. . . . Olympic organizers in London planned to protect London from conventional terrorism. But of all the things they might have thought might happen, I'd be surprised if civil insurrection was high up on their list of expected risk factors."[10]

The knotty problem, however, is that the Olympics aren't a parallel operation to mass civic unrest; they are an aggravator. "Youth clubs and libraries are being shut down as expendable fripperies; this expenditure, though, is not negotiable," wrote British novelist China Miéville in the New York Times Magazine. The Olympic torch may as well be an instrument of arson—because, as Miéville notes, "the uprisen young of London . . . do the math."[11]

Ask the residents of Clays Lane Estate, in East London. After World War II, Britain made public housing (what is called council housing) a right, not a "handout." Clays Lane Estate was the largest housing cooperative in the UK and the second largest in all of Europe. Over the past few decades, however, this once-proud tradition has been systematically eroded. Now the country is facing a shortage of affordable housing as rents climb and the poor are pushed out. "The banlieuefication of London," Miéville writes, in reference to the poor, isolated, heavily policed neighborhoods outside Paris, "is under way."[12]

At the same time, the construction of gleaming corporate headquarters and architectural showpieces in London has proceeded apace. Now on the skyline: state-of-the-art Olympic facilities and ominous military structures designed to intimidate all into submission. Amid protests, Clays Lane Estate was demolished to make way for yet another piece of the grand Olympics plan. The peaceful gatherings and protests were ignored, and as a result we get riots—what Dr. Martin Luther King so insightfully called "the language of the unheard."

But even as London burned, much of the political class chose to hear nothing. Boris Johnson, the Tory mayor who edged out Red Ken in his reelection bid, rushed back from vacation to say, "In less than 12 months we will welcome the world to a great summer Games in the greatest city on earth—and by then we must all hope that we will look back on these events as a bad dream." Categorizing it as a "bad dream" is another way of being oblivious. Former Olympic great (and current Olympic flack) Lord Sebastian Coe even called everything that week "business as usual."[13]

But many others are far less confident. Paula Radcliffe, the women's world record holder in the marathon, said, "In less than one year we welcome the world, and right now they don't want to come."[14]

The London games of course went off without a hitch. After all, the city has more security cameras per capita than anywhere on earth. It also has a militarized police force, a compliant media, and a political establishment that, no matter the party, has a finger in the pot and some skin in the game. The question was whether the IOC would itself demand an even more severe police crackdown to ensure that the games would run according to plan.

When reached for comment, a representative of the IOC told me that they will stay completely out of any security arrangements. Andrew Mitchell, media relations manager of the IOC, e-mailed, "Security at the Olympic Games is a top priority for the IOC. It is, however, directly handled by the local authorities, as they know best what is appropriate and proportionate. We are confident they will do a good job in this domain."

This assertion has left many rolling their eyes. Bob Quellos, an organizer for No Games Chicago, which helped keep the Olympics out of the Windy City for 2016, said to me, "Simply, what the IOC wants, it gets. In London next summer, the IOC will be dictating the level of police repression. Billions of dollars have been spent on the security. London's Olympic Park is already a highly militarized zone protected by barbed wire, dogs, and armed patrols."

Chris Shaw, the author of *Five Ring Circus: Myths and Realities of the Olympic Games,* pointed out, based on his experience in Vancouver during the 2010 winter games, that the harassment would only get worse: "[As the games approached] the Charter [the Canadian bill of rights] went out the window for the duration of the games; people were followed and harassed. Reporters were deported and cops were acting like reporters."

This has certainly been the case for previous Olympic festivals, as well. Every historical precedent points to an increased crackdown in the months ahead, which will only fan tomorrow's flames.

As of this writing, there were to be at least 14,500 British troops in the UK for the Olympics, more than are stationed in Afghanistan. Beyond that, there were to be at least 10,000 private guards and contractors, and the esteemed Royal Navy's largest battleship was to be docked in Greenwich to safeguard the equestrian events. Bomb-disposal units, helicopters, fighter jets, and ground-to-air missiles were to be on standby. There was also going to be a unit known as the "brand police," there to make sure that no one is sneaking any merchandise into Olympic venues that isn't pre-approved.

As the costs continued to spiral, in a time of brutal cuts, there was no guarantee of anything except more conflict to come.

Len McCluskey, leader of the country's largest union, Unite, raised the possibility of strike action during the Olympics. In an interview with the *Guardian,* McCluskey said that the attacks on public-sector workers were "so deep and ideological" that they had every right to target the games. "The idea the world should arrive in London and have these wonderful Olympic Games as though everything is nice and rosy in the garden is unthinkable," he added. "Our very way of life is being attacked. By then, this crazy health and social care bill may have been passed, so we are looking at the privatisation of our National Health Service." McCluskey also urged the public to engage in "all forms of civil disobedience within the law."[15] The city's bus drivers voted by 90 percent to strike during the games, unless they are compensated for the extra work involved. They won the extra pay, but both sides walked away from the negotiating table gnashing their teeth.

We have a collision coming between post-Olympic London and the poor, angry youth of Great Britain—one that is all but ensured if David Cameron's ultimate response continues to be "Let them eat beach volleyball."

Vancouver

For anyone in London or Brazil who believes that the Olympics are a smooth operation, remember this from 2010: winter Olympics officials in tropical Vancouver were forced to import snow—on the public dime—to make sure that the games could proceed as planned. This use of tax dollars was just the icing on the cake for angry Vancouver residents. Unlike the snow, that anger still simmers two years after the fact.

When I arrived in Vancouver several weeks before the start of the games, the first thing I noticed was the frowns. The International Olympic Committee had leased every sign and billboard in town to broadcast Olympic joy, but they couldn't pay the local populace to crack a smile. It's clear that the 2010 winter games had darkened the mood in the bucolic coastal city. Even the customs police officer checking my passport started grumbling about "five-thousand-dollar hockey tickets."

Polls released on my first day in Vancouver backed up my initial impression. Only 50 percent of residents in British Columbia thought that the Olympics would be positive, and 69 percent said too much money was being spent on the games.[16]

"The most striking thing in the poll is that as the Olympics get closer, British Columbians are less likely to see the Games as having a positive impact," said Hamish Marshall, research director for the pollster Angus Reid. "Conventional wisdom was that as we got closer to the Olympics, people here would get more excited and more supportive."[17]

If the global recession hadn't smacked into planning efforts the previous year, with corporate sponsors fleeing for the hills, maybe the Vancouver Olympic committee would have found itself on more solid ground with residents. But public bailouts of Olympic projects when people see their own jobs and social safety net slashed are hard to swallow.

I spoke to Charles, a bus driver, whose good cheer diminished when I asked him about the games. "I just can't believe I wanted this a year ago," he said. "I voted for it in the plebiscite. But now, yes. I'm disillusioned." This disillusionment grew as the financial burden of the games was increasingly revealed. The original cost estimate was $660 million in public money. At the time of my visit, it was at an admitted $6 billion and steadily climbing. An early economic-impact statement was that the games could bring in $10 billion—but PricewaterhouseCoopers had just released their own study showing that the total economic impact would be more like $1 billion. In addition, the Olympic Village came in $100 million over budget and had to be bailed out by the city. As for security, the estimated cost was $175 million. At that point, it was already clear that the final cost would exceed $1 billion.

These budget overruns were coinciding with drastic cuts to city services. On my first day in town, the cover of the local paper blared cheery news about the games on the top flap, with a smaller headline announcing the imminent layoff of eight hundred teachers much farther down the page. As a staunch Olympic supporter, a sports reporter from the *Globe and Mail,* said to me, "The optics of cuts in city services alongside Olympic cost overruns are, to put it mildly, not good."

But to Vancouver residents—particularly those living in the downtown east side, the most impoverished area in all of Canada— these weren't just PR gaffes. Carol Martin, who worked in the blighted neighborhood, made this clear: "The bid committee promised that not a single person would be displaced due to the games, but there are now three thousand homeless people sleeping on Vancouver's streets and these people are facing increased police harassment as they try to clean the streets in the lead-up to the games."

When I explored the back streets of the east side of downtown, I found police congregated on every corner, trying to hem in a palpable anger. Anti-Olympics posters plastered the neighborhood, creating an alternative universe to the cheery 2010 games displays by the airport. The Vancouver Olympic Committee tried to quell the crackling vibe by dispersing tickets to second-tier Olympic events like the luge. It wasn't working.

Officials were feeling the anger, and the independent media, frighteningly, paid the price. In November 2009, *Democracy Now!*'s Amy Goodman was held while driving across the border. She was traveling to Canada for reasons that had nothing to do with the Olympic Games. In an interview with CBC News, Goodman recalled that the border agent's prime concern was whether Goodman would be discussing the Olympics. When she insisted that the Winter Games were nowhere on her mind, they detained her anyway. After leaving detention, Amy Goodman had a new curiosity in the goings on.

As Derrick O'Keefe, co-chair of the Canadian Peace Alliance, said to me, "It's pretty unlikely that the harassment of a well-known and respected journalist like Amy Goodman . . . was the initiative of one overzealous, bad-apple Canadian border guard. This looks like a clear sign of the chill that the IOC and the games' local corporate boosters want to put out against any potential dissent."

In 2010, Martin Macias Jr., an independent media reporter from Chicago, was also detained and held for seven hours by Canada Border Services agents. Macias, who was twenty years old at the time, is a media-reform activist with community radio station Radio Arte, where he serves as the host/producer of *First Voice,* a radio news zine. I spoke to Macias, and his account was chilling:

> I was asked the same questions for three and a half hours in a small room. They told me I had no right to a lawyer. I went from frustrated and angry to scared. I didn't know what the laws were or how the laws had been changed for the Olympics. I kept telling them I wasn't going to Vancouver to protest but to cover the protests, but for them that was one and the same.

To add insult to injury, Canadian authorities then deported Macias and insisted he pay his own way out of the country. "They wanted me to buy a thirteen-hundred-dollar plane ticket back to Chicago. I said, 'No way,' and now I'm in Seattle." Macias's story is not unique. Two delegates aiming to attend an indigenous assembly held alongside the games were also detained and turned away.

For those with just a passing knowledge of our neighbors to the north, this must all seem quite shocking. When we think of human rights abuses and suppression of dissent, Canada is hardly the first place that comes to mind. But Canada has its own history of cracking down on peaceful protesters, as anyone who attended the 2001 Free Trade Area of the Americas demonstrations in Quebec will attest.

But the people of the downtown east side and beyond developed a different outlet for their Olympic angst: a full-scale protest to welcome the athletes, tourists, and foreign dignitaries. Vancouver residents put out an open call for a week of antigame actions, organizing demonstrations on issues ranging from homelessness to indigenous rights. Protesters from London and Russia, sites of the next two Olympics, joined in. Tellingly, polls showed that 40 percent of British Columbia residents supported the aims of the protesters, compared to just 13 percent across the rest of Canada. Activist and author Harsha Walia said to me, "We are seeing increasing resistance across the country as it becomes more visible how these games are a big fraud."

The games also coincided with the largest and longest-standing annual march in Vancouver: the February 14 Women's Memorial March, which calls attention to the hundreds of missing and murdered women (particularly indigenous women) in British Columbia. The Vancouver Olympic committee asked the Memorial March organizing committee if they would change the route of the march for the Olympic Games. As Stella August, one of the organizers with the downtown east-side Power of Women Group, said to me, "We are warriors. We have been doing this for nineteen years and we aren't going to bow down to the Olympics."

But it's not just the Olympics. All international sporting events tend to act as neoliberal Trojan horses, preying on our love of sports to enforce a series of policies that would in any other situation be roundly rejected. Nowhere have I seen this more clearly than in South Africa in 2010, before the country's historic turn as host of the most popular tournament on earth.

South Africa's *Invictus* in Reverse

You see it the moment you walk off the plane: a mammoth soccer ball hanging from the ceiling of Johannesburg international airport, festooned with yellow banners that read, "2010 Let's Go! WORLD CUP!" If you swivel your head, you see that every sponsor from Coca-Cola to Anheuser-Busch has joined the party and branded its own banners with the FIFA seal.

When your head dips down, you see another, less sponsored universe. Even inside this state-of-the-art airport, men from the ages of sixteen to sixty ask if they can shine your shoes, carry your bags, or even walk you to a cab. It's the informal economy fighting for breath under the smothering cloak of official sponsorship.

Welcome to South Africa, a place of jagged contrasts: rich and poor, black and white, immigrant and everyone else. On a normal week, it's the dispossessed and the self-possessed fighting for elbow room. Racist apartheid, as many are quick to point out, has been supplanted with "economic apartheid," a reality visible throughout the country, if you choose to see it. It is not uncommon, but always entirely tragic, to hear black South Africans reflect on how some parts of their lives were easier under apartheid. Under apartheid there was a welfare state. There was employment. There was massive state intervention in the economy. The white minority in power made these investments to stave off inevitable social unrest. Today, it's a free marketeer's paradise. These are the normal conditions, the normal contrasts. But the 2010 World Cup took these contrasts and inflated them to the bursting point.

The lead-up to the World Cup in South Africa could best be dubbed *"Invictus* in reverse.*"* For those who haven't had the pleasure, the 2009 film *Invictus* tells of how Nelson Mandela used sports, particularly the nearly all-white sport of rugby, to unite the country after the fall of apartheid. The World Cup, in contrast, provoked efforts to camouflage every conflict and present the image of a united nation to the world. As Danny Jordaan, the World Cup's lead South African organizer, said, "People will see we are African. We are world-class."[18] Note that the concern is about what the world sees, not what South Africans see. What South Africans see, as one young man told me, is "football looting [their] country."

The contrasts became conflicts because the South African government, at the behest of FIFA, was determined to put on a good show, no matter the social cost. Thousands had been displaced, forced from their homes into makeshift, tin-roofed shantytowns, to make way for stadiums and make sure that tourists could avoid unseemly scenes of poverty. The United Nations even issued a complaint on behalf of the twenty thousand people removed from the Joe Slovo settlement in Cape Town, called an "eyesore" by World Cup organizers. The homeless were packed into guarded settlements hundreds of miles from the action. As Johannesburg councilor Sipho Masigo said about the removal of the poor, "Homelessness and begging are big problems in the city. You have to clean your house before you have guests. There is nothing wrong with that."[19]

There was also a heavy crackdown on those who make their living selling goods by the stadiums. Regina Twala, who had been vending outside soccer matches for almost forty years, was told that she and others had to be at least one kilometer from the stadiums at all times. "They say they do not want us here," Twala told the *Sunday Independent*. "They do not want us near the stadium and we have to close the whole place."[20]

To make matters worse, FIFA pushed the South African government to announce that they would arrest any vendors who tried to sell products emblazoned with the words "World Cup" or even "2010." One young woman, whose mother worked in a clothing factory, told me of the factory manager looking on hurriedly to make sure that "2010" didn't find its way onto any of the labels. In addition, any local beers, soft drinks, or fast foods not branded with the FIFA label could not be sold if they were in close proximity to the stadiums. A once-vibrant landscape of small shops selling locally made artisanal goods and food became dotted with fast food chains common in any American suburb. The stadium areas started to resemble the Green Zone in Iraq. Samson, a trader in Durban, said to me, "This is the way we have always done business by the stadium. Who makes the laws now? FIFA?"

Samson was only referencing the threats toward vendors, but his criticism was equally valid against the series of legal ordinances South Africa passed to prepare for the tournament. Declaring the World Cup a "protected event," the government, in line with FIFA requirements, passed bylaws that "spell out where people may drive and park their cars, where they may and may not trade or advertise, and where they may walk their dogs." They've made clear that beggars, or even those caught using foul language (presumably off the field of play), could be subject to arrest.

Then there were the assassinations. In a story that made international news but gained next to no notice in the United States, two people (on a discovered list of twenty) were assassinated for "whistle-blowing" on suspected corruption in the construction of the $150 million Mbombela Stadium. The *Sunday World* newspaper

attained the list, which included two journalists and numerous political leaders. Accusations swirled that the list was linked to the
ruling African National Congress (ANC), which the ANC has denied in somewhat bizarre terms. "The ANC wants to reiterate its
condemnation of any murder of any person no matter what the motive may be," said ANC spokesperson Paul Mbenyane.[21] It's never
a good sign when you have to make clear to the public that you are
staunchly opposed to murder.

To add to this specter of political violence, an extremist right-
wing, white supremacist organization, the Suidlanders, was found
to be stockpiling arms in advance of the tournament. After the April
2010 murder of white supremacist leader Eugene Terre'Blanche,
the Suidlanders held meetings around the country and encouraged
people to boycott the World Cup in solidarity with their cause.
"The time has come for people to realise they cannot be on the
sideline any longer and everybody's participation is needed to defend the last bastion of a true Christian nation against total annihi-
lation," said the statement on their website. While no violence took
place at the hands of the Suidlanders, the fear factor enhanced the
ANC's efforts to create a security state.

All of this—displacements, crackdowns on informal trade, the
rise of a terrorist white majority, even accusations of state-sponsored
assassinations—echoes the days of apartheid. Responsibility for
this state of affairs falls firmly on the shoulders of FIFA, but also on
the ANC. After all, South Africa's turn hosting the World Cup was
meant to bolster both "brands." I saw this firsthand when I took a
private tour of the breathtaking $457 million Moses Mabhida Sta-
dium in Durban, South Africa. I left the stadium utterly stunned,
for better and for worse.

Named after the late legendary leader of the South African Communist Party, the stadium is a stylistic masterpiece. The eggshell-

white facility is visible for miles, its milky waves rising from the earth in sharp contrast with its dusty, urban environs. The open roof has a graceful, slender arc connecting one side of the stadium to the other. The arc itself is a wonder: it starts as one clean curve, then splits into two separate stretches of white. This is an homage to the post-apartheid South African flag, the stripes symbolizing, as the government website states, "the convergence of diverse elements within South African society, taking the road ahead in unity." Well-heeled adrenaline junkies can even go to the top of the arc and bungee-swing across the pitch. Unity is now a thrill ride for the benefactors of the post-apartheid regime

On one side of the stadium, behind the goal, is a completely open vista through which the Durban skyline is majestically welcomed into the stadium. But the true engineering achievement of Moses Mabhida Stadium is the bleachers. They angle up with such subtlety that the effect is of a saucer instead of a bowl. Each of the 74,000 seats has a picture-perfect sight line on the action, whether you are in the nosebleeds or the corporate boxes. The seats themselves are painted in rich colors: the first level is royal blue to represent the ocean, the middle one is green to signify the land, and the top is brown, as a sportswriter said to me, "so it looks full on television." (Sure enough, filling the stadium, and all the new stadiums, in the two years since the World Cup has been a quixotic effort.)

The most striking color in the stadium is not in the bleachers, though. It's the grass, which is a green so bright it hurts the eyes, as if every blade were painstakingly colored with a Magic Marker. The shade was achieved with the aid of near-infinite gallons of crystal-clear water, which I saw constantly irrigating the field.

I raise the issue of the stadium's incomparable beauty because South African politicians in support of the World Cup accused detractors of what they called "Afro-pessimism." They alleged that critics lacked the faith that South Africa could host an event of this magnitude. They held up the steady stream of racist invective in the European press about the "looming disaster of the South African World Cup" and implicated any critics, no matter their motives. If the World Cup "lost," they argued, then Africa would also lose.

But this was an argument aimed at squelching dissent, not challenging European prejudice. When a country already dotted with perfectly usable stadiums spends approximately $6 billion on new facilities, that's an unconscionable squandering of resources no matter the continent. The situation grows even more egregious when 48 percent of South Africans live on less than 322 rand (about $42) a month.[22]

Back at the stadium, it became clear that the health of the grass took precedence over the health of South Africa's poor. In townships across the country, lack of access to water spurs regular protests. As Simon Magagula, who lives in a mud house near one of the new stadiums, said to the *New York Times,* "We've been promised a better life, but look how we live. If you pour water into a glass, you can see things moving inside."[23]

To see an architectural marvel like Moses Mabhida Stadium in a country where so many lack access to basic, affordable shelter is to witness government interests colliding with those of the citizens they've been elected to serve. And for such a stadium to be named in honor of Moses Mabhida, who symbolizes antipoverty struggles for millions of South Africans, is to stare at irony in its most lurid form.

As the price and the demands made by FIFA grew more onerous, many South Africans did have second thoughts. Zayn Nabbi, a sports correspondent for South Africa's E Television who gave me the stadium tour, said, "We were all so caught up in the love story of winning the World Cup—the romance of it all—we didn't grasp or we weren't told the repercussions. We all got caught up in the spin. I put myself in that category certainly. The hangover when this is all done will be brutal, man."

But the hangover started before the party ended, as these stark contrasts provoked fierce, wholly predictable resistance. In a normal month, South Africa has more protests per capita than any nation on earth. During the World Cup crackdown, the numbers skyrocketed. Over seventy thousand workers took part in strikes connected to World Cup projects since the preparations began, with twenty-six strikes since 2007. A woman named Lebo said to me, "We have learned in South Africa that unless we burn tires, unless we fight police, unless we are willing to return violence on violence, we will never be heard." Patrick Bond, from the Centre for Civil Society in Durban, noted that protests should be expected: "Any time you have three billion people watching, that's called leverage."

The struggles on display put the word *"ubuntu"* to the ultimate test. *"Ubuntu"* is a treasured Bantu term roughly translated as "unity." But unity doesn't quite do it justice. Liberian peace activist Leymah Gbowee defined it as a concept meaning, "I am what I am because of who we all are." [24] During South Africa's decades-long struggle against apartheid, *"ubuntu"* meant unity of purpose of the country's black majority and allies against a brutally oppressive regime. It meant the assertion of humanity in the face of an inhuman system.

The sacred word resurfaced, unsurprisingly, amid South Africa's lead-up to the 2010 FIFA World Cup. This time, though, *"ubuntu"* was used quite differently in speeches and rallies held by the ruling African National Congress. It still meant "unity," but it was cheapened to a pep talk. It was also used against people who dared ask uncomfortable questions. As Saleh, a youth activist in Johannesburg, said, "If someone stood up at a [council meeting] and said, 'Why are we spending so much on stadiums? Why are we giving the police so many powers?' we were told that we were violating the spirit of *ubuntu.*" His friend Peter chimed in: "The World Cup is like a marvelous party, but what happens the next day when we're hungover and the bill comes due?"

Although the *ubuntu* soured far sooner than anyone could have predicted, the 2010 World Cup was without question a major sporting success for South Africa. The gleaming fields opened on schedule, new airports welcomed scores of visitors, and with cameras ready to catch it, disparate groups of South Africans who usually self-segregate exulted together in public.

But the party's over. In the aftermath, the country was hit with massive strikes involving 1.3 million public-sector workers, including teachers, civil-service workers, and health workers. The response to the public-sector strike was particularly shocking for South Africans and international observers alike. When striking workers marched through a police line while sounding the World Cup's iconic *vuvuzela,* they were assaulted with rubber bullets.[25]

The strikes, as well as the rapid-fire erosion of the World Cup's *ubuntu,* speak to a serious political crisis facing South Africa's scandal-plagued president Jacob Zuma. They also reveal deep fissures between the ANC government and its base of support. The ANC has benefited greatly from its reputation as the freedom fighters who led South Africa's struggle against apartheid. But after sixteen years, in today's South Africa, 1.9 million people, or 15 percent of the total population, live in shacks. More than half of eighteen-to-twenty-five-year-olds are unemployed, with unofficial numbers likely much higher. Rates of rape and violent crime keep climbing. This all while the top twenty paid directors at companies listed on the Johannesburg Stock Exchange make 1,728 times the average income of a South African worker.

For a nation forged in a struggle against injustice, this situation is intolerable. The ANC depends on a tripartite alliance between themselves, the South African Communist Party, and the Congress of South African Trade Unions (COSATU), which is behind the recent strikes. If you're a part of the new black middle class, one of the "Black Diamonds," as they're known, you probably have a positive view of the party. If you live in the townships or are a young member of COSATU and your existence has been defined by economic apartheid, it's not enough. Indeed, now the ANC finds itself in direct conflict with the very unions that traditionally comprised its spine.

A resurrection of *ubuntu* is surely on the agenda in South Africa. But it's an *ubuntu* that could leave the ANC out in the cold—that could well take form *against* the ANC—as South Africa's youth and its workers demand economic justice and strive to reclaim their country.

There is a scene in *Invictus* where Morgan Freeman's Mandela says, "I thank whatever gods may be for my unconquerable soul. I am the master of my fate." Indeed, the people of South Africa consider themselves unconquerable whether they face apartheid, FIFA, or their current government.

By insisting on the notion of sports as an apolitical space, we do a great disservice to those facing the realities of the "event sports." People face very real police abuses, displacement, and onerous taxation. Media outlets do their best to not discuss it so as not to ruin the big party. If we don't talk about these issues, Brazil will continue paying a terrible price.

In the poem "Invictus," in which Mandela found so much inspiration, William Ernest Henley writes,

Beyond this place of wrath and tears
Looms but the Horror of the shade,
And yet the menace of the years
Finds, and shall find, me unafraid.

It's a poem about taking control of one's own destiny no matter the obstacles. Mega sporting events shape the economic, political, and personal destinies of masses of people with zero accountability for their trail of displacement, disruption, and destruction. People in Brazil are already showing themselves to be "unafraid" as they attempt to master their fate. They will remind the world that the party has a price.

·4·

Zombie Teams and Zombie Owners

The headline in March 2012 was as thrilling as the man himself: "Magic Johnson buys Los Angeles Dodgers for $2 billion." You don't know which part of that newsflash to start with first. Like one of his signature no-look passes, it commands immediate attention and turns your head.

There's that price tag of two billion dollars, the highest amount ever paid for a pro sports franchise. There's the fans' relief that the Dodgers, buried under the dubious accounting practices of former owner Frank McCourt, also known as "Frank McBankrupt," would finally be on secure financial ground. But most of all, there is Magic himself.

Just as he, along with Larry Bird, helped transform the NBA from something destitute to a feel-good global brand, the Magic man would now try to do the same for the Dodgers. Magic would be the king of Los Angeles, rehabilitating a team whose reputation had been shredded in the eyes of the local populace and had the previous year fallen short of three million ticket sales for the first time in two decades. This headline also holds the promise of history. In buying the team of Jackie Robinson, Magic would be desegregating the ownership suites of Major League Baseball.

But like a Magic pass, this headline also holds its share of misdirection. The real players behind the curtain are a financial services firm called Guggenheim Partners. The general managing partner of the team, the true owner, is Guggenheim CEO Mark Walter. "Mark Walter buys Dodgers" is a decidedly less flashy headline.

We don't actually know how much of his own money Magic paid. This is because Major League Baseball and the Dodgers are classified as private companies and are under no obligation to disclose the details. This is in itself criminal given the billions of public dollars larded into MLB coffers for the construction of new ballparks. The Dodgers have also received a flood of public funds to refurbish their own stadium. They also took public funds last year to pay the LAPD to take over stadium security after a San Francisco Giants fan was almost beaten to death in an unlit and unsupervised parking lot.

Most likely, Magic is a figurehead on a purchase that looks worse the further you look beyond that billion-dollar smile. Guggenheim Partners is counting on securing a massive new cable television contract to pay back their costs. According to the *Los Angeles Times,* this will mean higher cable bills for all Angelenos, baseball fans or not. In other words, the cost of buying the Dodgers will be passed on to the already cash-strapped city of Los Angeles. The real buyers are not Magic and the Guggenheim Partners; they are the people of Los Angeles, most of whom will never set foot inside the stadium.[1]

Magic now joins a fraternity of sports owners who are in a state of profound denial. For a generation, they have fed on public subsidies, sweetheart cable deals, and luxury box seats at the expense of the typical fan. Now, with tightening budgets and a public less willing to entertain owners' pleas for public funds, they are sitting on top of a financial sports bubble.

How the Bubble Is Still Blowing Up

Sports, so long a symbol of community cohesion, has become a symbol of community neglect. There was a time when the team bonded families, friends, neighbors, and strangers together. It was the symbol of unification at the heart of a city. Now when many of us see the local stadium, we see a $1 billion real estate leviathan where we cannot even afford to take our families and that was paid for with our tax dollars. When we see failing schools, crumbling roads, or shuttered community centers, we can look at the stadium on the skyline and see a "sports shock doctrine" at work.

Three years ago, former Michigan governor Jennifer Granholm described General Motors as "a health care provider that happens to make cars."[2] For more than a generation, many sports franchises have been highly leveraged urban or suburban real-estate developments where people happen to play games. A tour of the cradle of U.S. manufacturing—Cleveland, Milwaukee, Detroit, Oakland, and Pittsburgh—would find new, publicly funded stadiums that generate little more than underpaid service industry jobs. These jobs are part of a broader, less stable, less secure urban landscape across the country, where people are fighting to keep their heads above water. This dynamic has created a new species of fan: those who are paying for the stadiums but, unless they are working behind a counter, are unable to enter their gates.

Some owners are still extracting public wealth to build stadiums: the Minnesota Vikings, the Miami Marlins, and the San Francisco 49ers, oblivious to state budgets, have secured billions in corporate welfare. And, in many cases, new sports facilities still have a hold on local elected officials. As *Field of Schemes* author Neil deMause writes, "Because team owners can choose new cities but cities can't choose new teams . . . mayors feel they must offer owners anything they want or risk a voter backlash."[3] Grease the right politicians and a publicly funded stadium can still be yours.

In these tough economic times, however, more owners have attempted to adjust to the new financial realities by engaging in bitter labor battles in baseball, basketball, and the NFL—essentially, trying to extract wealth from players to make up for stadium subsidy shortfalls. As NFL commissioner Roger Goodell wrote in an open letter to fans,

> Economic conditions . . . have changed dramatically inside and outside the NFL since 2006 when we negotiated the last CBA. A 10 percent unemployment rate hurts us all. Fans have limited budgets and rightly want the most for their money. I get it. . . . Yes, NFL players deserve to be paid well. Unfortunately, economic realities are forcing everyone to make tough choices and the NFL is no different.[4]

His final analysis: the league will be mired in crisis unless greedy players play longer for less.

This entire situation might seem difficult to comprehend. After all, how could a global, twenty-four-hour entity described as "having a license to print money" possibly be in trouble? How can owners who have either made or inherited billions of dollars claim that they need public money or their businesses will go under? Make no mistake, some of this is creative accounting. Antitrust exemptions have given all sports leagues myriad ways to mask their books and tell players and municipalities that they are losing money, with the hope that everyone will take them at their word.

Major League Baseball documents that were leaked in 2010 showed the national pastime to be an unaccountable, highly secretive legal monopoly that willfully misrepresents the bottom line. They revealed, for instance, that despite protestations of perpetual

poverty, the Pittsburgh Pirates have made a fortune while not field-
ing a winning team in nineteen years. Pirates owner Robert Nutting
pulled $29.4 million in profits in 2007 and 2008 despite fielding
losing teams with a $23 million payroll, the lowest in the game. As
long as he receives revenue from big-market clubs via the luxury tax
and extorts millions in revenue from the Pirates' publicly funded
home at PNC Park, he couldn't care less.[5]

But the worst story to emerge from the MLB documents is that
of the then-Florida—now Miami—Marlins, owned by multimil-
lionaire art dealer Jeffrey Loria. The Marlins built a stadium that
will cost the public two billion dollars over the next forty years, all
while lying about their bottom line to max out their corporate welfare potential. As Yahoo! sportswriter Jeff Passan wrote,

> The team fought to conceal the $48.9 million in profits
> over the last two years because the revelation would have
> prompted county commissioners to insist the team provide
> more funding. Loria, an art dealer with a net worth of hun-
> dreds of millions, wouldn't stand for that. He wanted as much
> public funding as possible—money that could've gone toward
> education or to save some of the 1,200 jobs the county is
> cutting this year.[6]

In response, Yahoo! sportswriter Patrick Hruby invoked the Occupy movement:

> Sick of corporate bailouts? Occupy the Marlins. Tired of see-
> ing your hard-earned tax dollars line the pockets of people
> already in the top one percent of income earners, such as
> Goldman Sachs executives and team owners and goateed
> closers? Occupy the Marlins. Looking to take a stand against
> the ever-escalating cost of being a sports fan, ever-escalating

government spending or the ever-escalating sense that
wealthy special interests are taking the general public for a
ride? Occupy the Marlins.[7]

The Marlins were "bailed out." But how do you bail out an entire league? The 2011–12 National Basketball Association season
almost didn't happen because of what NBA commissioner David
Stern called "a crisis of profitability." Stern claimed throughout negotiations that twenty-two out of the thirty teams had lost money
the previous year and that the league held a debt of 300 million
dollars. But in earlier years, the NBA had extended lines of credit
to teams that risked being unable to make payroll. Stern's claim
was contested. In an independent forensic autopsy of the league,
Forbes tallied the number of troubled teams at seventeen and stated
that the league had actually made money. The league tersely re-
torted that *Forbes* was wrong—that a magazine that once trum-
peted the slogan "Capitalists of the World Unite" was just part of
the media effort to vilify the 1 percent. At the same time, the billionaire owners were crying poor over contracts no one had forced
them to sign; they were the "wronged billionaires."

The "wronged billionaire," who is just trying to create jobs while
also carrying our economy, is one of the most chutzpah-infused
public relations creations in recent memory. As one "wronged billionaire" owner, Washington Wizards owner Ted Leonsis, wrote
in a blog post called, "Class Warfare—Yuck!," "Economic Success
has somehow become the new boogie man . . . anyone who has
achieved success in terms of rank or fiscal success is being cast
as a bad guy in a black hat. This is . . . really turning off so many
people that love America and basically carry our country on their
paying taxes and by employing people and creating GDP."[8]

Ted Leonsis happens to be one of the owners who claimed financial losses, but he left out a few details. There's a reason why he is

a billionaire. To create the Verizon Center in the heart of DC's Chinatown, residential housing was razed, businesses were shuttered, and families were priced out of the neighborhood. Now, instead of Chinese families, there are Starbucks and Chipotles with Chinese characters above their blaring signage. As for "carrying the country" on his back, Leonsis might want to thank his army of minimum-wage Verizon Center workers for keeping his ample frame in fitted suits.

The owners of the NBA and David Stern have repeatedly failed to remain accountable to the communities they've raided and to the players they've happily put under contract. Author Malcolm Gladwell, who is no radical, ended his own column on the NBA lockout by writing, "We have moved from a country of relative economic equality to a place where the gap between rich and poor is exceeded by only Singapore and Hong Kong. The rich have gone from being grateful for what they have to pushing for everything they can get. . . . In the end, this is the lesson of the NBA lockout."[9]

No matter who you believed during the lockout, the root problem is obvious: NBA owners don't share the revenue produced from their local television contracts. In the NFL, teams from Green Bay can compete with teams from New York because owners are obligated to share television cash. The Los Angeles Lakers make as much money in one year from their local cable deal as the Portland Trailblazers make in ten. Knicks owner James Dolan can engage in a marathon run of bad free-agent signings and know that cable television money will bail him out. But challenging the power of his wealthiest patrons wasn't on Stern's agenda, so NBA owners solved their profitability crisis by demanding and receiving that three-billion-dollar transfer of wealth over the next decade from players to owners. As NBA player Etan Thomas, who is on the NBA Players Union executive committee, said to me, "The owners are speaking another language from us. They refuse to get their own house in order and don't want to negotiate as much as dictate." This should sting every player because after a year of record revenues, they should be earning more, not taking historic cuts.

Then there is the NFL. The most powerful league in sports, coming off the most watched Super Bowl in history, locked out its players and risked the 2011 season because they also claimed a crisis in profitability. Commissioner Roger Goodell said quite explicitly, "The current system threatens the future of the league." The owners demanded more money to make up for projected recession profit losses and that the players participate in two more games each season. In their justification for the lockout, the owners said explicitly that it was because they were getting far fewer subsidies for stadiums than they had expected. Then, in the same paragraph, they said that they were really doing it for the fans. Seriously. Roger Goodell, in a statement I'm sure he'd rather were forgotten, said, "We can't continue to shift the cost, whether it's the rising player cost or the rising cost of operating an NFL franchise, on to our fans. That's why we're trying to get a better economic model."[10] This was so illogical that *Washington Post* columnist Sally Jenkins said, "The NFL owes fans a season. Why? Because the fans paid for it, that's why, and this isn't 13th-century France." Continues Jenkins:

> Their world-view was summed up the other day by Dallas Cowboys owner Jerry Jones: "I just spent a billion dollars on a stadium, and I didn't plan on not playing football in it," he said. Now, that's a funny thing for Jones to say, because as it happens, he doesn't actually own Cowboys Stadium. The city of Arlington does. And Jones didn't spend a billion dollars to build it. Arlington taxpayers passed a bond issue and wrote him a check for $325 million. City sales tax increased

by one-half a percent, the hotel occupancy tax by 2 percent, and car rental tax by 5 percent, all of which may hurt the local economy. Jones is merely a tenant, with a lease.[11]

It's a terrible scam that has far more in common with the unaccountable corporate-welfare models that crushed the U.S. economy than a league just trying its darnedest to help the fans.

The two most egregious examples of how our broken economic system has spread its "vampire squid" tentacles into the world of sports are found in Major League Baseball, among the two wealthiest media markets in the United States: New York and Los Angeles. New York Mets owner Fred Wilpon and his partner Saul Katz bankrupted their franchise by using the team as an ATM to invest with, as well as loan money to, the disgraced and very imprisoned financier Bernie Madoff. On the opposite coast, Dodgers owner Frank McCourt became embroiled in the ugliest divorce this side of an MTV reality show. It was revealed that he used his team like a piggybank, underwriting a lifestyle that would make Caligula blush. McCourt couldn't even make his organization's payroll.

The two stories seem quite different, and Major League Baseball commissioner Bud Selig certainly treated them as such. The league extended credit to Wilpon, a longtime friend of Selig's, and forcibly seized the Dodgers from the arriviste outsider McCourt. But one ugly thread connects the two stories: a worldview that the 1 percent in this country feels will never change. For years, taxpayers, local governments, and their own players have bailed out the owners. But the real world caught up with Wilpon and McCourt. These cases revealed not just that McCourt would get $1,200 haircuts or that Wilpon thought to entrust Bernie Madoff with his team's future. They revealed, clearly and unapologetically, a glimpse of how owners put fans last.

The Coastal Meltdowns

Three years ago, at Fremont High School in South Central Los Angeles, I asked a room of fifty teenagers how many of them had ever been inside the legendary Dodger Stadium. One intrepid student raised his hand. If you want to understand why Major League Baseball had to seize the storied franchise, look no further than this—and also understand that this moment is easily replicated in cities across the country.

The Major League seizure of the Los Angeles Dodgers is more than just a comment on Frank McCourt's financial problems or his divorce drama. It's more than a black eye for the once-proud franchise of Robinson, Koufax, and Valenzuela. It's more than a stain on a franchise that, from 1973 to 1986, led the Major Leagues in attendance every season except one. It is a commentary on the rotten state of Major League Baseball and a trend line that is looking worse with time.

The young fans are disconnected from the game, and franchises flirt with insolvency. Even the L.A. chamber of commerce expressed fears that the team might not be long for Los Angeles. Although this might provoke cheers in Brooklyn, it would be a tragedy for the game.

Commissioner Bud Selig's unprecedented, jarring response of simply seizing the team can only be read as a panic move. Like someone who just throws out everything in the attic rather than sort through the debris, it reads like a reactive response: the McCourt divorce, the embarrassing inability of a Major League owner to meet payroll, and the need to bring in showboating former New York Police Department chief William Bratton as head of security at Dodger Stadium. It's long been said—whether about steroids, realignment, or the All-Star Game—that Bud Selig's nickname is "Mr. Reaction." This did nothing to allay that criticism.

And what does an insolvent Dodgers franchise say about the state of America in the twenty-first century? Maybe it says nothing at all. Maybe it's as simple as saying that Frank McCourt ran a civic institution into the ground. But that doesn't explain the broader economic crisis in the sport. It doesn't explain why the Texas Rangers in 2010, on the road to the World Series, had to be auctioned off at a bankruptcy sale. It doesn't explain why most games are crowds of the very young and very old. It doesn't explain why Selig, when he crows about baseball's rosy financial picture, sounds like he's living in the last days of disco.

But more than anything else, it doesn't explain how, of all teams, the Los Angeles Dodgers find themselves in this crucible of humiliation. The Dodgers are arguably the most culturally significant franchise in the history of American sports.

From their Brooklyn days, the Dodgers were the franchise of the immigrants, the strivers, the ones who thought the American Dream was there for those willing to scratch and bleed for it. They were able to maintain this persona even when they broke Brooklyn's heart and absconded for the Left Coast. Even after displacing the Chicano residents of Chavez Ravine, who had built "a poor man's Shangri-La," they were able to enter the hearts and homes of the Chicanos, Dominicans, African Americans, and Asians that make up Southern California. There are still older Chicano residents who will say, "You see second base? That's where I used to live."

It was the first, and certainly not the last, modern stadium land grab. But the team itself, built in Brooklyn and a symbol of a dynamic postwar multicultural melting pot, became irresistible. Going to Chavez Ravine in the 1970s and 1980s was to stand amid a crowd of a diversity that would shame the United Nations. The fans were the reflection of the multicultural mosaic on the field of play, and the Dodgers have always been baseball as baseball wants to be known: a melting pot that speaks to our best angels. Unlike the Yankees, who simply won with remorseless efficiency, the Dodgers were interested in building a more perfect union.

A "perfect union" was surely the goal of Frank and Jamie McCourt when they married in 1979. By 2009, they had announced their divorce. The proceedings also revealed a lavish lifestyle lived at the expense of the team: $74 million on four homes, a $12 million pool, a $10,000-a-month hairstylist, $225,000 for Jamie's monthly expenses, and finally, $20 million in attorney fees. "I became a caricature of myself—and I became a caricature of somebody who was uncaring—unfeeling—excessively living—bad guy—and that's just not who I am," McCourt told *Good Morning America*.[12]

Precisely because this team has always lived at the heart of the national zeitgeist, their bankruptcy should be seen as a brutal microcosm of the leveraged capital and dashed dreams that define the new century. Harold Meyerson wrote in the *Washington Post* that the Dodgers under McCourt represented "a particularly vicious form of capitalism that America has come to know too well the past few decades: a new owner takes over a venerable firm and extracts what he can for himself, decimating the company and damaging the community in the process."[13]

In as public a way as possible, they became the symbol of a reality we often turn to sports to escape. Author Alison Lurie once wrote, "as one went to Europe to see the living past, so one must visit Southern California to observe the future."[14] That future is now marked by income inequality on par with the Ivory Coast, Jamaica, and Malaysia. It's a place of fake riches and real pain. Official unemployment sits at 12 percent, with youth unemployment at 35 percent.

In such an environment, the team that was always supposed to represent the spirit of immigrant America now has a shrinking, demoralized base of support. Attendance has plummeted. Tailgating is dismal. After a brutal beating in the stadium parking lot on opening day, security is now run by the LAPD, which shadows every corner, making the Elysian Fields feel like occupied territory. Dodger Stadium is no longer the place where you take your kids on your day off.

Perhaps the most emblematic moment of this entire saga has been seeing the name Vin Scully on the team's list of creditors. The eighty-three-year-old Scully had been the Dodgers' announcer for sixty-two years. Starting in Brooklyn and following the team across the country, he has brought the exploits of Dodger greats like Roy Campanella, Don Drysdale, Orel Hershiser, and now Matt Kemp to life. As Meyerson wrote, "I've long believed that kids who grew up listening to Scully got at least a 30-point bump on their verbal SAT."[15] Under McCourt's leadership, Scully became just another person the Dodgers didn't have money to pay.

What does the Dodgers' bankruptcy say about today's America? Everything. But if the Dodgers are synonymous with decay, the Mets' situation says much more about how we got here.

Growing up in New York City, I was a Mets fan down to the marrow of my bones. I'd stand outside the old Shea Stadium, pleading for autographs, and eventually my baseball glove had more names on it than the cast on a third grader's broken arm: Mookie Wilson, Ron Darling, Kevin Mitchell—any Met who'd stop for me. My bedroom was a shrine to the team; posters of Darryl Strawberry, Dwight Gooden, and Keith Hernandez watched over me as I slept. I didn't know they all sniffed coke, but I wouldn't have cared. I loved those teams. I always talked about them using the pronoun "we," as in, "We are going to win it all this year."

That's why, for countless fans and me, this story has been painful like no other. The ugly truth has been unveiled. The Mets weren't my team, or New York City's team. They were Bernie Madoff's team.

There tragically is no criminal statute against using and abusing an entire fan base. We now know that the owners of the Mets, Fred Wilpon and Saul Katz, were financial partners with the Babe Ruth of swindlers, Bernie Madoff. They allegedly used Madoff's portfolio as a sort of personal bank, with the team as both collateral and cash register. They then had to fight off a $1 billion lawsuit issued by the Madoff victims' trust. As the victims' trustee, Irving Picard, stated, Wilpon and Katz "made so much easy money from Madoff for so long" that, despite the myriad red flags, they "chose to simply look the other way. . . . There are thousands of victims of Madoff's massive fraud. But Saul Katz is not one of them. Neither is Fred Wilpon."[16]

According to the lawsuit, Wilpon was using his Madoff-made gains to pay off as much as half a billion dollars in debt he accrued in building the team's (tellingly named) new stadium, Citi Field. Wilpon also admitted that his position as Mets owner provided him access to elite investing circles and increased the value of his own real estate development corporation. In response to Picard, Wilpon and Katz aren't giving an inch. Their spokespeople said in a statement, "The trustee's lawsuit is an outrageous 'strong arm' effort to try to force a settlement by threatening to ruin our reputations and businesses, which we have built for over fifty years."[17]

That statement and many others like it are up on the Mets' website, making it even harder as a fan to cordon off one's feelings for the team. ("To see business owners so misjudge their audience is solar-eclipse-black humor," Yahoo! sports columnist Jeff Passan wrote.[18]) Wilpon and Katz are now looking to sell anywhere from a 25 percent stake to the entire team, and one hopes they will. The team has already received a $20 million loan from Major League Baseball after running through the $75 million line of credit available to all teams in financial distress. And they owe their players, some of them disastrous signings, money that they are scrambling to find.

Mets Nation is owed something, too—probably community ownership of the entire team. Not just because their trust was so flagrantly violated, their blue and orange entangled in a Ponzi scheme, but because New York taxpayers paid for $200 million of the $600 million it took to build Citi Field. Why shouldn't the Mets then follow the model of the Green Bay Packers and allow fans to buy shares?[19] This is a model worth emulating, especially given the Packers' recent success. Imagine if every time you saw a kid in a David Wright jersey, you knew that the proceeds would help keep the city afloat. In these tough times, when tightening budgets have led to historic attacks on schools, hospitals, and public services, why shouldn't the Mets help subsidize our future? They'd just be returning the favor.

The same solution goes for Los Angeles. The answer isn't found in the glittering Hollywood Hills or on Wall Street, but in the sparsely populated tundra of Green Bay, Wisconsin. The NFL's Super Bowl–winning Green Bay Packers present an alluring alternative that couples winning with community connection. Not only has the Packers' home field been sold out for two decades, but also during snowstorms, the team puts out calls for volunteers to help shovel and is never disappointed by the response.

Could this work in Los Angeles with the Dodgers, or in New York City with the Mets? Would fan ownership also translate to a deeper connection between city and team? It's a tantalizing question. But without profound public and political pressure, it's doubtful that we will get the chance to find out. Considering the generations of civic love bestowed on these teams, the people of these two great cities certainly have a greater claim on them than Guggenheim Partners or the crippled Wilpon.

It's unlikely that Major League Baseball or the sclerotic Selig would want any of this. After all, since 1961, it's been written explicitly in the league's bylaws that fan ownership is as forbidden as spitballs or aluminum bats. Selig sees his number one job as protecting the profits and interests of ownership, not safeguarding the interests of the game. Proclaiming to the world that fans can own a team and owners are superfluous runs counter to Selig's very DNA. For this suggestion to gain much traction at MLB central would be near shocking. When Joan Kroc, the late owner of the San Diego Padres, tried to transfer control of the team to the city as an act of philanthropy, baseball blocked the transfer.

But I also didn't expect Los Angeles councilwoman Janice Hahn to step up to the plate and take up the cause. Hahn, the daughter of infamous as well as legendary former city supervisor Kenneth Hahn, is now a member of the U.S. Congress. After McCourt declared bankruptcy, Hahn issued the following statement:

> The Dodgers have been previously owned by FOX and the McCourt family, it is clear that the only ones who have the teams best interest at heart are the fans. If elected to Congress, I will introduce an amended version of the "Give Fans A Chance Act" which would allow Major League Baseball teams to be owned and operated by their fans, much like the Green Bay Packers are structured today.[20]

This is an idea whose time has come. Major League Baseball for years has relied on public subsidies to make mountainous profits, collectivizing the debt and privatizing the profits. But now, as our states face historic cuts, it's time for payback. Twelfth-grade L.A. public school teacher Sarah Knopp said to me, "Just a percentage of the revenue from merchandise sales could help save the hundreds of art and music teachers being pink-slipped right now.

Maybe Dodger revenue could help us to develop world-class sports programs, rather than cutting them."

The only way this option could be pursued is with a tremendous amount of pressure. This pressure must be of two kinds: popular, fan-based pressure on Major League Baseball and political pressure on—and through—elected officials in L.A. and New York. People should rally, fans should hold up signs, politicians should be questioned, and we should cast off our passivity and realize that, as fans, our teams—and our cities—hang in the balance.

· 5 ·

Joe Paterno:
Death, Remembrance,
and the Wages of Sin

Joe Paterno's most fervent supporters always described "JoePa" as more of an educator than a football coach. The Brown University graduate and English literature major, it was said, always pushed those around him to think and learn. Now, following his passing at the age of eighty-five in January 2012, Paterno will be remembered for suffering the most dramatic fall from grace in the history of American sports, a victim of his own nurtured legend— one built on more than unbeaten seasons, a record thirty-six bowl appearances, and showers of confetti. The now toppled statues of Paterno on the Penn State campus, the academic courses that bear his name, even the "Peachy Paterno" ice cream for sale at the campus creamery all point to one thing: Paterno was more than a coach, more than a teacher, even more than a man. He was Penn State. He was a campus Sun King who had too much love for the weight of the crown. The reverence many Penn State alumni have held for the man was rooted in a sterling standard of morality and ethics that became inseparable from the Nittany Lion brand as well as a very conservative ideal of Americana. As Aurin Squire wrote, "When Penn State won the NCAA championship in 1987, it was seen as a victory for the Constitution, flag pins, and whole milk."[1] This is why fall 2011's grand jury report accusing revered long-time assistant coach Jerry Sandusky of being a serial child rapist, and former FBI director Louis Freeh's July 2012 report about Joe Paterno's role in covering up these abuses, were so devastating to Paterno's entire legacy. JoePa, upon hearing from grad assistant Mike McQueary that he had witnessed Sandusky committing statutory rape in the showers, did everything—but only the minimum—required by law. He informed those above him, telling the head of campus police and the athletic director, both of whom as of this writing are now out of work and under indictment. In the eyes of the law he did nothing illegal. But according to our conception of who this man was supposed to be, there was no authority above Joe Paterno. There was instead an expectation that this man of integrity would not hesitate to meet far more than the minimum standards of legality. Is that fair? When it's your statue on campus and your name on the buildings, most would say hell yes.

When Freeh issued his July report and we learned there was evidence Joe Paterno knew about formal allegations against Sandusky as far back as 1998; or that when Sandusky was forced into retirement in 1999 he continued to be a presence on campus, in the locker room, and even on Joe Paterno's sideline with young children by his side; or that Paterno, well aware of every sick allegation, wanted Sandusky in 1999 to stay as "Volunteer Position Director-Positive Action for Youth," the buzz of damning questions rose to a din: How could JoePa have been content with silence, given the possibility that children continued to be at risk? Did Joe Paterno and the campus leadership care more about their brand than anything resembling human morality? Had abused children become, in the view of Penn State's leadership, an unfortunate collateral damage necessary to keeping the cash registers ringing? Was a football program that had become the economic, social, and cultural center of an entire region more important than . . . anything?

The conclusions were not kind. After decades of service, Penn State fired Paterno with a cold 10:00 P.M. phone call, causing a low-frequency campus riot. Since then, Penn State's leadership has gone out of their way to protect "the Nittany Lion brand" (their words). As it turns out, Joe Paterno himself was far less important than the house that Joe Paterno built.

Before his death, Paterno was able to give one last interview to the *Washington Post*'s Sally Jenkins. He defended himself by claiming confusion about the reports he was hearing about Sandusky because he'd "never heard of rape and a man." For a football coach who always took pride in his own worldliness and erudition, not to mention his decades of involvement with the Catholic Church, this, to be kind, strains credulity. He also, we now know, lied to Jenkins about what he knew and when he knew it. In his last days, Paterno, this man of character, was often sounding like just another character: the powerful individual corrupted by his own deification.[2]

In Paterno's own tragic words, though, he also "didn't know which way to go," and he wished he'd done more upon hearing the allegations against Sandusky. We can, I believe, understand that. We can understand how hearing that your colleague of decades is some kind of monster could produce confusion. We can understand why Paterno would only tell the campus authorities who had "more expertise" in handling these matters. We can strain to understand saying nothing over the years, perhaps assuming the matter was taken care of, as you see the accused rapist walk into your office, or arrive on your sideline holding a small child by the hand, or using the very showers where someone may have witnessed the rape of a ten-year-old boy. We can understand how a person could think,

"I told the campus police. I did what I legally had to do. And now I don't want to think about this ever again." We can understand it, but that doesn't mean we have to excuse it.

One powerful figure did a lot more than "excuse" Paterno. Following the death of JoePa, Phil Knight, the founder and chairman of Nike, emerged as the late Penn State coach's great defender. At a packed, televised memorial service, Knight eulogized Paterno and went on the attack against the media and Penn State's board of trustees:

> In the year in question he gave full disclosure to his superiors up the chain to head of campus police and president of the school. The matter was in the hands of a world-class university and by a president with an outstanding national reputation. Whatever the details of the investigation are, this much is clear to me. If there is a villain in this tragedy it lies in that investigation, not in Joe Paterno's response to it. [applause] And yet, for his actions, he was excoriated by the media and fired over the telephone by his university. Yet in all his subsequent appearances in the press, on TV, interacting with students, conversing with hospital personnel, giving interviews, he never complained, he never lashed out. Every word, every bit of body language conveyed a single message. "We are Penn State."[3]

The funeral crowd went wild, as if attending a pep rally. Even the evil media praised Knight for his strong words. Jena McGregor, a columnist for the *Washington Post,* wrote a piece titled, "At Joe Paterno memorial service, Phil Knight shows true leadership." This may be true—but it's leadership right off a cliff and into a moral abyss.

The celebration of Knight's message by McGregor and other

attendees is one reason why so many now see Happy Valley, Pennsylvania, as some kind of ethical Bizarro World. It also drowns out the thousands of Penn State students who held vigils on campus against child abuse, and the Penn State alums who said they were "sickened" by the allegations against Sandusky. Instead it gives weight to the minority of alumni and students who see Paterno—and, by extension, themselves—as the real victims in this saga.

What Phil Knight and those attracted to his brand of rhetoric don't understand is that it's not "the media" that enraged people against Joe Paterno and Penn State. It's the fact that we're human beings and the thought of a respected member of the community raping children makes all of us feel vulnerable in a very primal way. Maybe we were abused, or maybe we know someone who was abused. Maybe we have children and drop them off every day with seemingly responsible adults whom we trust with their care. The unspoken fear, that there is a Sandusky in every town collecting damaged childhoods like Hummel figurines, is terrifying. The idea that someone—anyone—could have stopped Sandusky and didn't in order to protect a university "brand" is infuriating. The stories of children being told by school guidance counselors to keep their mouths shut lest they hurt Penn State is beyond depressing. The fact that Joe Paterno, an avatar of moral righteousness, did the bare minimum in the face of such egregious crimes is for many a mark on his character so dark that it shadows decades of good works.

That's why the presence of Phil Knight, in particular, as a defender does Paterno an awful disservice. In Knight, we have someone whose company, despite efforts at reform, still uses child labor under abhorrent sweatshop conditions. Much of it is subcontracted so Knight can feign ignorance, but that's a legal loophole, not a moral one. Think about children as young as four or five in Pakistan on an assembly line. Think about a company that deliberately builds factories in countries under authoritarian regimes so that anyone who talks workers' rights, let alone unionization, would face harrowing consequences. Or just Google "Nike, Child Labor" and prepare to be assaulted with accounts of systematic abuse. Given this grave reality, Jerry Sandusky, if guilty of every charge, would have to live a hundred lives to ruin the number of childhoods spent stitching the Nike swoosh.[4]

In Knight, we also have someone who pays college coaches a fortune so "student-athletes" can wear and, by extension, advertise his products. We have someone who shovels millions to the University of Oregon football program's state-of-the-art equipment and facilities while the school endures terrible cuts. Knight, I would argue, represents the corruption of amateur sports—and, by the same token, the corruption of Joe Paterno and Penn State. By defending Paterno, Knight did little more than defend himself and the kind of moral relativism he's exported to campuses around the country. Thanks to people like Phil Knight, programs like the one at Penn State have become too big to fail and too big to derail.

The World Joe Made

In better times, Happy Valley was known as "the world Joe Paterno made." Stationed in an unlikely corner of a largely working-class region, Penn State grew one of the finest public universities in the country. For many, the engine of Penn State's progress was exemplified by its football program. Nittany Lions football regularly draws a hundred thousand fans to Happy Valley. It also produces $50 million in pure profit for the university every year and has been listed as the most valuable team in its athletic conference, the Big Ten. Another economic report showed that every Penn State game pumps $59 million into the local economy, from hotel occupancies to kids selling homemade cookies by the side of the road.[5]

Paterno took a football team and turned it into an economic life raft for an entire region. But it's not just about the yearly profits. Paterno's brand was used as a beacon of integrity that allowed the school to transform from just another state college into a multibillion-dollar research university. Paterno himself spearheaded this promise after Penn State won the 1986 national championship. He personally went to the board of trustees and scolded them for not capitalizing on the team's success. Then he headed the fundraising committee to do exactly that. In 1988, he spoke at the Republican National Convention, endorsing George H. W. Bush for president. His "brand" was far more than just a local phenomenon.[6]

One PSU student named Emily wrote the following to SI.com's Peter King after the allegations against Sandusky went public. "Truth is, if not for Paterno's philanthropy and moral code (until his fatal lapse of judgment), I and thousands of others wouldn't be here right now. If not for Paterno . . . Pennsylvania State might still be an agriculture school and State College might be lucky if there were a Wal-Mart within a 30-mile radius."[7]

Emily was not alone. "How can you victimize Joe Paterno?" has become a frequent refrain among the "Penn State family."

It's worth delving into the details so they aren't forgotten as the hagiography machine commences its efforts to save the brand. The grand jury summation describes one scene where Sandusky was caught raping ten-year-old "Victim Number 2 in the Penn State football team shower," by former Penn State quarterback and graduate assistant coach Mike McQueary. McQueary was "distraught" and "traumatized." Did he go to the police? No, he went to his father, a State College resident, who had his son go directly to Joe Paterno's home. Paterno immediately turned the matter over to Athletic Director Tim Curley and Gary Schultz, the senior vice president of finance and business who oversaw campus security. Curley and Schultz then conferred and acted. According to the grand jury report, they sat Sandusky down and said that he could no longer use Penn State football facilities while accompanied by the young people from his child services charity, Second Mile. That's it. (Curley and Schultz were charged with perjury and obstruction. Paterno was not, although based on the Freeh report, he may well have been if he had lived.)

Curley even admitted to the grand jury that he "advised Sandusky that he was prohibited from bringing youth onto the Penn State campus from that point forward." Yet reports immediately surfaced that Sandusky was on campus running a sleepaway camp for boys as young as nine years old as late as 2009. One alleged victim told the grand jury that Sandusky brought him to a Penn State preseason practice in 2007—a full nine years after Paterno was first made aware of the shower rape. This is why it's hard to stomach Paterno's stating, "If this is true we were all fooled, along with scores of professionals trained in such things, and we grieve for the victims and their families. They are in our prayers." The truth is, this is a case that moved past prayer and into the realm of criminal negligence.[8]

Then again, this is what happens when a football program becomes the economic, social, and spiritual heartbeat of an entire region. Joe Paterno was the personification of everything that made Penn State matter in football, in academics, and in much of the state. When something becomes that valuable, a certain mind-set kicks in: Protect JoePa. Protect Nittany Lions football. Protect the brand above all. In a company town, your first responsibility is to protect the company.

But Penn State never was an "outlaw program." It was what every school was supposed to aspire to become. Now every athletic director or school president has to reckon with the fact that they have been looking up to an institution that places such value on football that children can become collateral damage. Let JoePa's last teachable moment be this: If your football coach is the highest-paid, most revered person on your campus, you have a problem.

If your school wins multiple championships and a booster drops money to build a statue of the coach, tear it the hell down. And if you think children are being raped, the minimum just isn't good enough, no matter whether or not you wear a crown.

Raging for the Coach

The week Joe Paterno was fired, a riot hit the Penn State campus. As the students raged, I received a call from my mother. I told her I couldn't talk because there was a riot at Penn State. My mother, a peaceful soul, surprisingly said, "Good!" I asked her what possibly could be good about it and she said, "Given the way they covered up the abuse of all those children, maybe there should be a riot!" I had to explain to her that the riot wasn't about the kids. It was about the coach.

But this wasn't the only violent campus demonstration to take place that night. On the campus of Penn State University in State College, Pennsylvania, several hundred students rioted in anger after the firing of their coach. At the University of California at Berkeley, a thousand students who identified with the Occupy movement attempted to maintain their protest encampment in the face of police orders to clear them out.

At Penn State, students overturned a media truck, hit an ESPN reporter with a rock, and made several (highly futile) attempts to set aflame the very heart of their campus. The almost entirely male student mob was given space by police to seethe and destroy without restraint.

At Berkeley, the police had a much different response. Defenseless students were struck repeatedly with batons as police attempted to disperse their occupation by Sproul Hall, the site of the famed Mario Savio–led free-speech battles of the 1960s. A university that advertises its tradition of protest on its website had its own campus police force send its own students to the hospital.

Two coasts, two riots. A frat riot and a cop riot, each an indelible mark of shame on an institution.

The difference is that at Berkeley, the Occupiers—a diverse assemblage of students, linking arms—pushed back and displayed true courage in the face of state violence. They would not be moved. These students are a credit to their school and represent the absolute best of a young generation that is refusing to accept the world as it is.

At Penn State, we saw the worst of this generation: the flotsam and the fools; the dregs and the Droogs; young men of entitlement who rage for the machine.

No matter how many police officers raised their sticks, the students of Berkeley stood their ground, empowered by a deeper set of commitments to economic and social justice.

No matter how many children come forward to testify how Sandusky sodomized them on their very campus, the students protesting at Penn State also stood their ground. They stood committed to a man whose statue adorns their campus, whose salary exceeded $1.5 million, and whose name for years was whispered to them as if he were a benevolent Russian czar and they the burgeoning Black Hundreds. Theirs was a tragic statement that proud Penn State has been in the lucrative business of nursing Joe Paterno's legend for far too long.

I spoke to a student who was at Sproul Hall and another resident who was a bystander in State College. The word that peppered both of their accounts was "fear"—fear that those with the space and means to be violent (the police at Berkeley and the rioters at Penn State) would take it to, as Anne, a Berkeley student, said to me, "a frightening point of no return."

I would argue that this "point of no return" has been reached, spurred by that night's study in contrasts. November 9, 2011, was a generational wake-up call to every student on every campus in this

country. Which side are you on? Do you defend the ugliest manifes-
tations of unchecked power or do you fight for a better world with
an altogether different set of values? Do you stand with the rioters
of Penn State or do you stand with Occupiers of Berkeley? It's fear
vs. hope, and the stakes are a hell of a lot higher than a BCS bowl.

The Next Saturday

Following the riots, Penn State made an intense effort to put forth a
good public face for their game against Nebraska that coming Saturday. The show would go on—just days after the accusations went
public, Paterno was fired, and the students did their funhouse-
mirror version of burn baby burn. The crowd was told to swathe
themselves in blue, because, it was said, that is the color of child
abuse awareness (by sheer coincidence, it also happens to be the
Penn State color). The team linked arms emerging from the tunnel.
They dropped to a knee with their Nebraska opponents at midfield
before the game. Once again, broadcasters told us, "the players
were paying tribute to the victims of child abuse."[9]

We were told all of this, and I wish it were true. But the response to one thirty-four-year-old Penn State class of 2000 graduate, John Matko, makes it hard to believe. Matko was rightfully
distraught by the revelations against Paterno and those in charge
at his alma mater. He was livid that students had chosen to riot
on campus that week in defense of their legendary coach. He was
disgusted that the board of trustees had decided to go ahead with
Saturday's Nebraska game as planned. John Matko felt angry and
was compelled to act. He stood outside the stadium holding up two
signs. One read, "Put abused kids first." The other said, "Don't be
fooled, they all knew. Tom Bradley, everyone must go." (Tom Bradley was named the interim head coach before being summarily fired
at year's end.)[10]

Without a doubt, there was much conflicted and genuine

emotion on the field and in the stands that day. The sports media, however, chose to respond by painting over any shades of gray. The atmosphere was reported as "somber," "sad," and "heart-rending," as "the focus returned to the children."

But let's go back to John Matko, who stood with his signs behind a pair of sunglasses. He wasn't soapboxing or preaching, just bearing silent witness. It was an admirable act, but no one bought him a beer. Instead, beer was poured on his head. His midsection was slapped with an open hand. Expletives rained upon him. His signs were kicked to the ground and stomped. As the *Washington Times* wrote, "Abuse flew at Matko from young and old, students and alumni, men and women. No one intervened. No one spoke out against the abuse."

One disapproving student said, "Not now, man. This is about the football players."[11] And with those nine words, we see the truth about Saturday's enterprise. The pain was born of self-pity, not reflection; the grievers were the exposed, not the penitent. It was about the football program, not the children. Thousands were mourning the death of a jock culture that, somewhere along the line, had mutated into malignancy.

This malignancy was not restricted to the Sandusky scandal, nor had it emerged overnight. Looking back, there are moments that spoke of the scandals to come. In 2003, less than one year after Paterno was told that Sandusky was raping children, he allowed a player accused of rape to suit up and play in a bowl game. Widespread criticism of this move was ignored; later, Paterno's decision was justified when no charges were brought against the player in question.

In 2006, Penn State's Orange Bowl opponent, Florida State, sent home a linebacker after accusations of sexual assault. Paterno's response, in light of recent events, is jaw-dropping. He said, "There's so many people gravitating to these kids. He may not have even known what he was getting into, Nicholson. They knock on the door; somebody may knock on the door; a cute girl knocks on the door. What do you do? Geez. I hope—thank God they don't knock on my door because I'd refer them to a couple of other rooms."[12]

Joanne Tosti-Vasey, president of Pennsylvania's National Organization for Women (NOW), was not amused. With chilling prescience, Tosti-Vasey responded, "Allegations of sexual assault should never be taken lightly. Making light of sexual assault sends the message that rape is something to be expected and accepted." NOW called for Paterno's resignation and, short of that, asked to dialogue with Paterno and the team about the issue of sexual assault. Neither Paterno nor anyone in power at Penn State replied to NOW, let alone accepted the invitation.[13]

Then there is Vicky Triponey. She was brought in as a compliance officer for the school, and part of her job was to make sure that the football team adhered to the school's honor code. But the Happy Valley utopia was suffering a spate of players accused of and arrested for assaults, public drunkenness, and even a knife fight, with no charges brought. Triponey was going to clean up the team, in line with Joe Paterno's vision. There was just one problem: Joe Paterno. The coach told her in no uncertain terms that she could take her honor code and cram it. When Triponey complained to school administrators about the profane, condescending, and hostile manner in which she had been addressed by the coach, she was ignored and eventually quit her job.[14]

This is the world JoePa made. It's, like many college towns, a company town where moral posturing acted as a substitute for actual morality.

That Saturday, while Matko endured the physical and verbal rage of the PSU faithful, hundreds gathered around the still-standing Paterno statue outside the stadium, laying down flowers and gifts. The only person who seemed to get it was the head coach of Penn State's victorious opponent, Nebraska's Bo Pelini. To his credit, Pelini said that the "game shouldn't have been played. . . . It's about doing what's right in society. It's about doing what's right and wrong. . . . It is a lot bigger than football, the NCAA, the Big Ten and anything else."[15]

In such an atmosphere, seeing the players and fans gather to bow their heads and mourn at the game wasn't "touching" or "somber" or anything of the sort. It was just sad—because they still didn't get it. The pain might run deep in Happy Valley, but the cancer runs deeper. To really move forward, the malignancy must be removed. Fire everyone. Shut down Happy Valley football for a year. Rebuild a healthier culture. Do whatever you have to do to make sure that the world Joe Paterno made has seen its last day.

One thing is certain: we need coaches, educators, and teachers at our universities. We don't need benevolent dictators with clipboards. We don't need collegiate Sun Kings. We don't need coaches who look across their expansive campuses and say, *"L'école, c'est moi."*

Aftermath

I am all for exposing what was fraudulent about Joe Paterno. I am all for calling him out as someone who cared more about his football program than the welfare of endangered children. I am also in full agreement with Louis Freeh that one of the greatest problems the Sandusky scandal has exposed is "the culture of reverence for the football program that is ingrained at all levels of the campus community." Children were raped in the name of this monstrous "culture of reverence."

But the conclusions I draw from this sobering reality are profoundly different than those of the NCAA. The oversight body decided to weigh in on Penn State. They decided to punish the school with a $60 million fine, a four-year post-season ban, and the vacating of all wins from 1998–2011. NCAA President Mark Emmert said piously, "Programs and individuals must not overwhelm the values of higher education." It's not "the death penalty"—also known as the end of the football program— but it's life without the possibility of parole.

Emmert sounds righteous. He's also dead wrong. It's a farcical public relations move that distracts the public from actually holding to account those responsible for protecting Sandusky. This decision marked a stomach-turning, precedent-setting, and perhaps even lawless turning point in the history of the NCAA. The punishment levied by Emmert was nothing less than an extra-legal imposition into the affairs of a publicly funded campus. If allowed to stand, the repercussions will be felt far beyond Happy Valley.

Take a step back from the righteous rage and just think about what took place: Penn State committed no violations of any NCAA bylaws. There were no secret payments to "student-athletes," no cheating on tests, no improper phone calls, no using cream cheese instead of butter on a recruit's bagel, or any of the Byzantine minutiae that justify Mark Emmert's $1.6 million salary.

What Penn State did was commit horrific violations of criminal and civil laws, and it should pay every possible price for shielding Sandusky, the child rapist. This is why we have a society with civil and criminal courts. Instead, we have Mark Emmert inserting himself in a criminal matter and acting as judge, jury, and executioner, in the style of NFL commissioner Roger Goodell. As much as I can't stand Goodell's authoritarian, undemocratic methods, the NFL is a private corporation and his method of punishment was collectively bargained with the NFL Players Association. Emmert, heading up the so-called nonprofit NCAA, is intervening with his own personal judgment and cutting the budget of a public university. He has no

—

right, and every school under the auspices of the NCAA should be terrified that he believes he does.

Speaking anonymously to ESPN, a former prominent NCAA official said, "This is unique and this kind of power has never been tested or tried. It's unprecedented to have this extensive power. This has nothing to do with the purpose of the infractions process. Nevertheless, somehow [the NCAA president and executive board] have taken it on themselves to be a commissioner and to penalize a school for improper conduct."

Emmert justifies this by saying Penn State "lost institutional control" of the football program. Tragically, the opposite is the case here. There was so much control a serial child rapist was able to have his tracks covered for—at least—thirteen years. He is instead using this canard of "institutional control" to justify an abrogation of public budgets, public universities, and, most critically, public oversight. Or as Yahoo! Sports' Pat Forde said succinctly, "Emmert seems determined to go where no NCAA president has gone before."

The discussion we should be having is how to organize the outrage of the Penn State campus and the people of Pennsylvania to expel the entire Board of Trustees. Just as the statue of Coach Paterno came tumbling down in the name of turning the page at Penn State, the board should follow. We should be talking about how to push for a full investigation of Governor Tom Corbett and his own extra-slow-motion investigation of Sandusky when he was the state's attorney general. Former governor Ed Rendell, as a board trustee during Sandusky's continued presence on campus, should be subpoenaed as well. But instead, we get the maiming of Penn State's athletic budget for the grand purpose of turning Mark Emmert and the NCAA into something they have no legal right to be. Private, unaccountable actors have no business cutting the budgets of a public campus. This move by Emmert didn't bring justice to any of Sandusky's victims. It didn't help clean house at Penn State. Instead it was extra-legal, extrajudicial, and stinks to high heaven. If we really want to do something other than beat a dead Nittany Lion, we should call for the heads of the real enablers. We should call for the resignation of the Penn State Board of Trustees including Governor Corbett. We should call for the abolition of nothing less than the NCAA.

· 6 ·

The NCAA's "Whiff of the Plantation"

Academe, n.: An ancient school where morality and philosophy were taught. Academy, n.: A modern school where football is taught.

—Ambrose Bierce, *The Devil's Dictionary*

n a poll commissioned by *Sports Illustrated,* 85 percent of university presidents stated that they believe too much money is spent on athletics. In the same poll, only 14 percent said they believe that their school spends too much on athletics.[1] This is the culture of denial at the highest levels of higher education. At these same institutions, athletes are pampered and spoiled, creating a moral sewer of scandal and, over the last two years, an overwhelming argument for reform.

Last year, I visited the University of Oregon, a proud institution whose budget is being slashed to the bone. The state legislature hiked in-state tuition 9 percent and passed an 11 percent decrease in funding to the Oregon system for 2011 and 2012. Buildings are crumbling and the faculty and staff have been forced to take unpaid furloughs to make up for budget shortfalls.

Yet the school is not in a state of complete disrepair. Thanks to Nike's emperor-in-charge, Phil Knight, the school's athletic

department, particularly its football program, is flush with cash.
New training facilities and the latest in exercise equipment, including underwater treadmills for the football team, are just the
beginning. Forget Vegas, Atlantic City, or Monte Carlo. You haven't
truly seen excess until you've toured the new $41.7 million athletic
center. In the ground-floor bathrooms—which are inlaid with black
marble—a portrait of Phil Knight's wife, Penny, graces the wall. (I
am told, but cannot personally confirm, that a similar tribute to a
leering Phil Knight has been sculpted in the women's bathroom.) It
is also worth noting that I saw more of the center than any of the
university's faculty, who are not allowed above the first floor.

While Oregon's athletes are able to take a dump in royal sur-
roundings and find respite from their pesky professors, the right to
be pampered may be their only right. If an athlete at Oregon or
anywhere else gets hurt, there is no compensation. If he doesn't fit
into a playing scheme, even if he has a 4.0 GPA, his scholarship is
revoked. If his jersey is sold, he doesn't see a cent. If he wants to
take a class against the coach's wishes, he cannot. If he suffers concussions or becomes addicted to painkillers, the years of medical
aftereffects are his burden alone.

Welcome to the NCAA in the twenty-first century, about as corrupt and mangled an institution as exists on the sports landscape.
At palatial college stadiums across the country, players are covered
in more ads than stock cars and generate billions of dollars, all to
the roar of the millions for whom college sports are tantamount to
religion. One problem cannot be tackled without the other: the
same system that spends so much on revenue-producing sports and
excuses the most egregious of scandals also exploits athletes to a
degree that renders such scandals inevitable.

A constant refrain by the yipping heads of the sports world is
that the NCAA is on a toboggan ride toward change. Certainly, a
slew of scandals and financial disasters make the need for reform

all the more urgent. Athletic departments, they say, can no longer function in their current form. An NCAA report showed that only fourteen of the hundred and twenty Football Bowl Subdivision schools made money from campus athletics in the 2009 fiscal year, down from just twenty-five the year before. In our time of austerity, public universities preach, with a catch in their throat, that the revenue just isn't there. Schools are "realigning" into different mega-conferences with the hope that this will provide enough money to keep them going. But even the revenue-producing sport of football loses money. We are told that change is coming in the NCAA, yet the past year tells a different story.[2]

Given the grim budgetary realities that surround state universities today, the numbers boggle the mind. According to USA Today, salaries of new head football coaches at the 120 bowl-eligible schools increased by 35 percent in 2011. Average pay has now ballooned to $1.5 million annually, an increase from $1.1 million. Over the last six seasons, football coach salaries have risen by an astonishing 55 percent. This has happened as tuition hikes, furloughs, and layoffs have continued unabated. In an era of stagnating and falling wages, compensation for coaching a college football team traces a trend line that rises like a booster's adrenaline during bowl season. The question is how—not just how this is possible given the stark economic realities of most institutions, but how schools can be this shameless.[3]

Justice-Curious?

Last April 2011, NCAA president Mark Emmert seemed to support the idea of reform. In an interview with USA Today, he said that at the NCAA annual board meeting he would "make clear . . . that I want [paying players] to be a subject we explore."[4] This came on the heels of an interview on PBS's Frontline special "Money and March Madness," where a scarlet-faced, visibly agitated Emmert refused to reveal his own seven-figure salary on camera and insisted that it would "be utterly unacceptable . . . to convert students into employees. . . . I can't say it enough, obviously. Student athletes are students. They are not employees."[5]

After Emmert revealed that he was "justice-curious," the NCAA quickly issued a statement that this kind of "exploration" was consistent with previous statements.[6] Sure enough, the April meeting produced a proposal for a stipend that was then quickly rescinded. The idea, though, that this was business as usual in the deluxe office complex that houses the nonprofit NCAA strains belief. In fact, it was yet another indication, just in time for the NCAA finals, that we seem to have reached a tipping point on the issue of compensating NCAA athletes for the billions they generate. As former Syracuse all-American linebacker Dave Meggyesy said, "These are more than full-time jobs. When I played at Syracuse in the early sixties, it wasn't like that. We had a regular season and twenty days of spring practice. Now it's year-round. It's a more cynical system now than when I played, starting with those one-year renewables. That's a heavy hammer. You get hurt, tough shit, you're out. And there's no worker's comp for injuries."

The block to reform is that, even as schools are losing money, even as "student-athletes" put themselves at risk for free, those in power have never had it better. March Madness, the NCAA's sixty-eight-team elimination basketball tournament, generates 96 percent of the NCAA's operating budget, including the salaries of fourteen vice presidents who make at least $400,000 a year. There are the brand-new $50 million, 116,000-square-foot headquarters in Indianapolis. Then there are the video games, posters, jerseys, and boutique credit cards featuring images of your favorite amateur athletes.[7]

And what about the college sports media industry? Over the last decade, the number of college football and basketball games broadcast on ESPN channels has skyrocketed from 491 to 1,320.[8] Besides, ESPN happens to be both the number one broadcaster of college football and basketball and the sport's number one news provider. This creates an atmosphere where covering sports and shilling for the industry are carnally intertwined. ESPN journalists reportedly show up to the Fiesta Bowl one week in advance, where they stay at the finest resorts and every day receive a different expensive present courtesy of the tournament's sponsors. As DC radio host Steve Czaban said, "It sounds like sports-media Chanukah." The Fiesta Bowl was found to have been an embezzlers' paradise for years with no one the wiser. Then there is the March Madness basketball tournament on CBS—and its neat $1-million-per-commercial rates in the Final Four. Eight hours of coverage and many commercial breaks later, there is the cure for the media recession blues.[9]

I haven't even mentioned the multibillion-dollar gambling industry. March Madness is now officially a busier time in Vegas than the Super Bowl. No other event unites sports fans with non–sports fans in offices and factory break rooms quite like it. Every year, overheated articles from the business press rail about work productivity lost to the annual rite of filling out your brackets. Over $100 billion passes through Sin City at that time—chicken feed compared to the money changing hands under the table and online.

For the student-athletes, however, there is simply nothing. As Dale Brown, former LSU coach, said, "Look at the money we make off predominantly poor black kids. We're the whoremasters."[10] Desmond Howard, who won the 1991 Heisman Trophy while playing for the Michigan Wolverines, called the system "wicked," telling USA Today, "[you] see everybody getting richer and richer. And you walk around and you can't put gas in your car? You can't even fly home to see your parents?"[11]

This is indeed a civil rights issue, a fact that was made manifestly clear by the great chronicler of the civil rights movement, Taylor Branch. Branch is the Pulitzer Prize–winning author of a mammoth three-volume series on the life of Dr. Martin Luther King Jr. But he also has some roots in the sports world, as the co-author of Bill Russell's memoir, *Second Wind.* In October 2011, in an article for the *Atlantic,* "The Shame of College Sports," he sparked a discussion only amplified by the recent scandals. As Branch wrote,

> My research for The Atlantic story led me to question and finally reject only the NCAA's right to impose amateur rules on college players without their consent. Contrived monopoly is a formula for exploitation, economic and otherwise, as sadly evident in the unfolding criminal scandal at Penn State. . . . The tip system has become harder to defend in lavishly commercialized college sports. By excluding players from basic rights, the NCAA concentrates power unchecked in college athletic departments, where coaches have the gall to say they must keep the money for the players' own good, to protect the amateur purity of youth.[12]

As a fresh set of eyes from outside the sports world, Branch succeeded in pointing out what many of us see every day but have become too callous, too jaded, or too bought-off to notice. While college presidents cry about athletic department deficits, Branch pointed out that in 2010, the Southeastern Conference (SEC) "became the first to crack the billion-dollar barrier in athletic receipts. The Big Ten pursued closely at $905 million. That money comes from a combination of ticket sales, concession sales, merchandise, licensing fees, and other sources—but the great bulk of it comes from television contracts." He pointed out the existence of ESPNU, a channel dedicated to college sports, and that Fox Sports was developing something similar. He noticed that Auburn's

Heisman Trophy–winning quarterback Cam Newton wore at least fifteen corporate logos—"one on his jersey, four on his helmet visor, one on each wristband, one on his pants, six on his shoes, and one on the headband he wears under his helmet"—as part and parcel of Under Armour's $10.6 million deal with the school.[13]

Dr. King's biographer looked at all this and could come to only one conclusion:

> For all the outrage, the real scandal is not that students are getting illegally paid or recruited, it's that two of the noble principles on which the NCAA justifies its existence— "amateurism" and the "student-athlete"—are cynical hoaxes, legalistic confections propagated by the universities so they can exploit the skills and fame of young athletes. . . . The NCAA makes money, and enables universities and corporations to make money, from the unpaid labor of young athletes.[14]

Branch, whose civil rights credentials are above reproach, added that

> Slavery analogies should be used carefully. College athletes are not slaves. Yet to survey the scene—corporations and universities enriching themselves on the backs of uncompensated young men, whose status as "student-athletes" deprives them of the right to due process guaranteed by the Constitution— is to catch an unmistakable whiff of the plantation.[15]

We have reached a clear sense of exhaustion with the injustice of it all and the steady monotony of these scandals. It's time for a change. Former all-American and NBA star Jalen Rose offered a concrete proposal, writing, "[The] overwhelming time commitment of practice, film sessions and team obligations make it impossible to maintain a part-time job, which is not permitted. It's difficult to juggle two full-time jobs—going to school and playing athletics. A $2,000 per semester stipend would go a long way for giving the student athletes extra money to help pay bills and living expenses."[16]

I would add that all NCAA athletes—whether or not they're in a revenue-producing sport—should have their scholarships guaranteed if they maintain their grades. In the current system, coaches renew scholarships on an annual basis. If you get hurt or don't fit into a coach's system, you are yesterday's news.

The arguments against issuing a stipend—or work-study—to scholarship athletes tend to wither at the slightest touch. Critics point out that the players get free room and board, which should be enough, or that paying them would ruin their "spirit" and "love of the game." As one author noted, "To provide recompense would be to degrade [them] toward a spiral of barbarism. [In the current system] they are cared for and governed in a way that allows them to be supervised instead of being thrown to the wolves."

Apologies. That last quote wasn't from a defender of the current scholarship system but from George Fitzhugh, the nineteenth-century Virginia writer whose defense of slavery, *Cannibals All! or, Slaves Without Masters,* argued the moral benefits of well-supervised bonded labor.[17]

This comparison to the old South is echoed by the current system's most prominent critics, and not just those branded "outsiders" like Taylor Branch. Walter Byers, the executive director of the NCAA from 1952 to 1987, and the man most responsible for the modern NCAA, has seen the light. He said to the great sportswriter Steve Wulf, "The coaches own the athletes' feet, the colleges own the athletes' bodies, and the supervisors retain the large rewards. That reflects a neoplantation mentality on the campuses."

The old justifications are sounding as antiquated and offensive as George Fitzhugh.[18]

The hard truth, obvious to everyone not suckling at the NCAA's teat, is that all the soul-searching is a fraud. Despite the fact that more than three-fourths of college presidents know that intercollegiate sports is not sustainable, they treat football like a prize pig to be protected at all costs. Ohio State University, one of the schools so marred by scandal, recovered nicely by hiring former Florida head coach Urban Meyer for $24 million over six years. That's a base salary of $4 million a year. In 1982, his last year as a head coach, legendary Buckeye football coach Woody Hayes made $42,000. (Before the scandal became too much to bear, Ohio State president E. Gordon Gee said, on the prospect of firing Jim Tressel, "No, are you kidding me? Let me be very clear. I'm just hoping the coach doesn't dismiss me."[19]) After Penn State hired New England Patriots assistant Bill O'Brien to replace Joe Paterno, O'Brien fired more than a half dozen assistants—and placed a cool $4.4 million in severance pay on the public university's payroll.[20] For all the scandal, the Ohio State and Penn State football programs are some of the precious few that propel their athletic departments toward positive total revenue. But the trickle stops at the gym's doors. As it turns out, positive athletic revenue and an engorged athletic budget offer little to the rest of campus. Just look at the most lucrative football school in the land, the University of Texas.

There is no state in the union more synonymous with football than Texas. From the Dallas Cowboys to *Friday Night Lights,* pigskin has long defined the Lone Star State. Yet one group is determined that, in a time of serious economic crisis, football know its place: the faculty at the University of Texas, Austin. Following an undefeated season and a trip to the 2012 Bowl Championship Series national championship, the University of Texas System Board of Regents upped coach Mack Brown's total compensation from

$3 million to $5 million a year. In response, the Faculty Council voted to condemn the raise as "unseemly and inappropriate."[21]

Why would the council criticize a raise for the man who led UT football to national glory and millions of dollars in television, alumni, and bowl revenue?

Here's why. At a time when Texas football is doing quite well, the rest of the campus is tightening its belt. The UT Tuition Policy Advisory Committee has recommended that undergraduate tuition increase 4 percent each year for the next two years—nowhere near as bad as the 32 percent increase at the University of California, but in a recession that's small comfort. Departments across the campus are feeling the pinch and being asked to make significant budget cuts. Layoffs and hiring freezes have been announced in several departments. At every turn, academic priorities have found themselves, for lack of a better term, sidelined.

Predictably, the sports media have been out front and center defending these priorities. On his radio show, former Washington Redskins All-Pro LaVar Arrington reminded the faculty, "Hundreds of thousands of people don't show up to watch you teach." In an article subtly titled "Texas Head Coach Mack Brown Deserves His Two Million Dollar Raise," Bleacher Report's Edwin Bear wrote, "The Texas football program brought in a nationwide record $87 million in 2008. To add Texas' football program channeled $6.6 million into UT's academic programs in recent years, according to UT's president William Powers Jr. in an ESPN article. (By the way how awesome is the last name Powers esp when he's the president where he works?!)" Yes. It's so awesome, it almost makes up for the fact that the school is raising tuition and cutting salaries to the bone.[22]

Bear's analysis also gives the impression that surpluses are a fact of life at top football programs. Hardly. "College sports is widely viewed as an out-of-control train on a collision course with academia," said David Hillis, a professor of integrative biology, to the *Austin American-Statesman.* "Right now, UT is stoking this train to make it run ever faster."[23]

For most schools, this isn't close to the case. Far more typical is the situation at the University of Maryland, where former coach Ralph Friedgen was paid $2 million to go home and numerous teams were cut from the athletic department. Meanwhile, new football coach Randy Edsall is banking over $3 million while presiding over a losing program that has repelled boosters, harmed ticket sales, and led to an exodus of his best players, including his quarterback, ACC freshman of the year Danny O'Brien. Hiring Edsall to revive the football program was a huge gamble, as is all of modern college football: push your chips into the middle of the table and hope for the best. For the college presidents crying poor while continuing to pay these salaries, the complaints are pathetic, and the comparisons to Wall Street are obvious and unflattering.

But whether a school is generating revenue or going bankrupt, the coaching arms race continues. Penn State emeritus professor John Nichols, chair of the Coalition on Intercollegiate Athletics, a faculty group advocating for athletics reform, said of the wage hikes, "This just shows . . . the difficulty of bringing [football] into the right proportion, the right balance with the academic mission."[24] That a Penn State professor said this only speaks to the problem. The reformists inside the NCAA are like members of Alcoholics Anonymous who gather at an open bar.

A century ago, the great intellectual (and sports fan) W. E. B. Du Bois wrote about the corrosive effect college athletics was beginning to have on the health and culture of academic institutions. If schools are reduced to football factories where classes just happen to be taught, everyone loses, particularly the unpaid athletes who generate millions and are told they are being paid with academics. Without the academics, they nakedly become chattel, delivering a new contract for their coach and a whole lot of school spirit without even the pretense of a functioning college to attend in return.

These are tough times, and it's in tough times that we turn to our sports teams for a sense of pride, hope, and accomplishment. But this is really a question about the future of higher education. For a generation, universities have been increasingly organized to deliver a profit, and the notion that these are institutions where learning should be valued for learning's sake has become quaint. The gears of the machine are moving ever faster in the wrong direction. It is high time we lie upon them, or we'll face a future with football on Saturday followed by six days of manufactured ignorance.

Just like anger about Wall Street excess only became productive when several hundred occupied Zuccotti Park, change to the NCAA—whether it's paying players, reining in coaches' salaries, or challenging the reign of King Football—will only happen if students, professors, and players take this decision out of the hands of their school presidents and into the campus square. Unfortunately, nowhere is the gap between words and deeds more clear than in the NCAA itself.

Scandals reign across the college landscape, and every time the NCAA gets to play the cop. But in reality, they are more like Tony Soprano: dispensing harsh judgments, putting down recalcitrant underlings, and, more than anything else, making sure everyone still gets paid on schedule, all while adhering to a moral code that's paper thin and painfully transparent. Positioning the NCAA as a moral arbiter only perpetuates the "gutter economy," and we are all the worse for it. Shutting the NCAA down would end the culture of corruption once and for all.

But this won't happen by accident. It will only happen if college athletes move from complaining about their situation to action. Taylor Branch told the following remarkable story in his piece on the NCAA:

William Friday, the former North Carolina president, recalls being yanked from one Knight Commission meeting and sworn to secrecy about what might happen if a certain team made the NCAA championship basketball game. "They were going to dress and go out on the floor," Friday told me, "but refuse to play," in a wildcat student strike. Skeptics doubted such a diabolical plot. These were college kids—unlikely to second-guess their coaches, let alone forfeit the dream of a championship. Still, it was unnerving to contemplate what hung on the consent of a few young volunteers: several hundred million dollars in television revenue, countless livelihoods, the NCAA budget, and subsidies for sports at more than 1,000 schools. Friday's informants exhaled when the suspect team lost before the finals.

There is really only one thing that could actually stop the madness in its tracks.

I'm often asked what a twenty-first-century "Tommie Smith/John Carlos moment" would look like. In today's far more demonstrative, flamboyant sports world, it would take a hell of a lot more than just players raising their fists. NCAA athletes would need to not merely appropriate the style of Smith and Carlos but accomplish their ends: waking us up to a thriving injustice, risking their livelihoods, and pissing off fans, network executives, and their own coaches in one fell swoop. It would require them to walk to midcourt before the Final Four, or midfield before the national championship game, ripping off their assorted brands and logos, and state in no uncertain terms that unless they get a piece of the pie, they are walking off the field. The fans would boo. The announcers would rage. The coaches would fume. But they would be revered by history. The next Smith/Carlos moment is there for any student-athlete willing to grasp it.

·7·

Here Come Los Suns

The rise of anti-immigrant hysteria, from Washington, DC, to Wasilla, Alaska, has recently found resistance in the most unlikely of places: the world of sports. It all started in Arizona, a state that has become ground zero for every anti-immigrant wingnut law on the wish list of the radical right. These wishes were granted in April 2010, with the passage of the Support Our Law Enforcement and Safe Neighborhoods Act (SB 1070). One Democratic lawmaker said that it has made Arizona a "laughing stock"[1]—but it's difficult to find an ounce of humor in this vile piece of legislation. The law makes it a crime to walk the streets without clutching your passport, green card, visa, or state ID. It not only empowers but absolutely requires police officers to demand paperwork if they so much as suspect a person of being undocumented. A citizen can, in fact, sue a police officer for failing to harass suspected immigrants. The bill also makes it a class-one misdemeanor for anyone to "pick up passengers for work" if their vehicle blocks traffic. And a second violation of any aspect of the law becomes a felony. As Jon Stewart said, Arizona has truly become "the meth lab of American democracy."

In response to SB 1070, Arizona representative Raul Grijalva called for a national boycott against the state, urging Americans to forgo vacationing or retiring there. Most people repulsed by this legislation, however, didn't find themselves in either vacationing or retirement mode. They did, however, live in baseball cities where the Arizona Diamondbacks would come to play.

It just so happens that D-backs owner Ken Kendrick is a massive financial supporter of Arizona's state Republican Party, so his team is as legitimate a target as any. In 2010, the National Republican Senatorial Committee's third-highest contributors were the executives of the Arizona Diamondbacks. The team's big boss, Ken Kendrick, and his family members, E. G. Kendrick Sr. and Randy Kendrick, are dutifully following in the footsteps of team founder and former owner Jerry Colangelo, another big donor and bundler. Along with other baseball executives and ex-players, Colangelo also spearheaded a group called Battin' 1000, a national campaign that uses baseball memorabilia to raise funds for Campus for Life, the largest antichoice student network in the country. Colangelo was also deputy chair of Bush/Cheney 2004 in Arizona. His deep pockets created what was called the Presidential Prayer Team, a private evangelical group that claims to have signed up more than one million people to drop to their knees and pray daily for Bush.[2]

Under Colangelo, John McCain also owned a piece of the team. Before the passage of SB 1070, the former maverick said that he "understood" why it was being passed, because of "the drivers of cars with illegals in it [that] are intentionally causing accidents on the freeway."[3]

Kendrick denied his support of SB 1070. Yet he also held fundraisers in his owner's box during D-back games for SB 1070–supporting politicians. Leave aside, for a moment, the ethical and perhaps legal ramifications of raising money for pet candidates in a stadium built with 250 million in public dollars. The fact remains that while Kendrick publicly distanced himself from the controversial bill, he was perfectly comfortable using the home of the supposedly "apolitical" Diamondbacks organization as a fundraising center.[4]

This is who the Arizona Diamondbacks executives are. This is the tradition they stand in. The Diamondbacks' owners have every right to their politics; after all, if we were to police the political proclivities of every owner's box, there might not be anyone left to root for (except, of course, for the Green Bay Packers). But SB 1070—basically an open invitation to racial profiling and harassment—is too much to abide.

The D-backs thus became the SB 1070 Traveling Road Show, with protests in Chicago, Houston, Atlanta, Florida, Colorado, and San Francisco in May 2010 alone. Overall, demonstrations were staged in more than twenty cities, with one common goal: to move the 2011 All-Star Game out of Arizona.[5]

The ballpark protests were not just a response to Kendrick's political proclivities. Marching at the ballpark nationalized an issue many on the anti-immigrant right would rather see tucked away in the shadows of the Southwest. Fittingly, the first ballpark protests were held at Chicago's Wrigley Field, where people had picketed and petitioned to integrate Major League Baseball in the 1930s. One particularly smart element of the Chicago protest was that picketers did not ask fans to walk away from the stadium. Considering that most of us buy our tickets in advance, this could have backfired. Instead, organizers asked fans to go inside and hold up signs calling for the repeal of SB 1070 during the game.

The San Francisco demonstration was particularly notable, with a thousand people and a lead banner that read "Racists are Worse than Dodgers' Fans."

In DC, a large ballpark protest was publicly threatened by a pugnacious anti-immigrant organization called Help Save Maryland. They threatened to "swamp" the demonstration and drive immigrant-rights supporters from the park; they brought seven people. The demonstration outside was combined with actions inside the park, where four daring activists stormed the field with one out in the fifth inning and unfurled a banner calling for Selig to move the game. In what became a YouTube sensation, an overzealous security guard attempted to accost them and did a less-than-graceful belly flop across the outfield.[6] It might have been the most exciting moment at a Nats game in the 2010 season. As the four on the field were being arrested, two separate banners with similar messages were draped over the outfield walls. These banner bandits, who dared display a message that didn't say "Drink Budweiser" or "Buy Season Tickets," were banned from the ballpark for a year.

Rosa Lozano, who spent the evening in custody for taking the movement to the outfield grass, said to me after her release, "I did it because when history reflects this egregious time of civil and human rights violations I want to be able to have pride in saying that I didn't stand idly by and allow human beings to be treated like animals because of their immigration status." Another activist, Brian Ward, added, "I find it funny how I am being banned from a stadium that I helped pay for with my tax dollars. I say if that is what it takes to get the All-Star Game moved, let's all do actions like we saw today and show that we are willing to do whatever it takes to move this game and overturn SB 1070."

Outside the park, some fans were very supportive, even joining in with the chants and marching around in full Nationals gear calling for the All-Star Game to be moved. Others yelled and heckled with all the zeal of Michele Bachmann at a book burning. Two demanded to see the papers of a seventeen-year-old picketer, Nate Taitano, who happened by sheer and utter coincidence to have brown skin. Most critically, thousands of fliers detailing how people could contact Bud Selig were passed out. By day's end, protesters were soaked, hoarse, and happy. As Gary Nelson, a firefighter from

Baltimore who drove an hour to be at the demonstration, said, "Evil flourishes when good people do nothing. Today we did some good."

The two dozen ballpark protests also inspired baseball players themselves, historically some of the most conservative and reticent pro athletes, to speak out. At first, Major League Baseball's Latino players were deafening in their silence. Considering that 27.7 percent of MLB players are Latino, the question lingered: would anyone say anything against the law, or are Latino players, as all-star Gary Sheffield infamously remarked in 2007, aggressively recruited precisely because they can be "controlled"?[7]

Well, SB 1070 opened the floodgates. Kansas City Royals DH José Guillén said, "I've never seen anything like that in the United States, and Arizona is part of the United States. I hope police aren't going to stop every dark-skinned person. . . . It's just crazy we're even talking about this." Dodgers first baseman Adrian Gonzalez, then playing for the San Diego Padres, added, "It's immoral. They're violating human rights. In a way, it goes against what this country was built on."[8]

Venezuelan-born San Diego catcher Yorvit Torrealba agreed with Gonzalez, saying, "This is racist stuff. It's not fair for a young guy who comes here from South America, and just because he has a strong accent, he has to prove on the spot if he's illegal or not. I mean, I understand the need for security and the safety to people here, the question of legal and illegal. I get that. But I don't see this being right. . . . I come from a crazy country. . . . Now Arizona seems a little bit more crazy."[9]

Marlins manager Ozzie Guillén (no relation to José), also Venezuelan, said he would boycott the 2011 All-Star Game "as a Latin American" if it went ahead in Phoenix as planned. "The immigration [service] has to be careful about how they treat people . . . ," he said, adding, "I want to see this country two days without [immigrants] to see how good we're doing."[10]

It wasn't just Latino players and coaches speaking out. Michael Young, of the Texas Rangers, added, "You can quote me. It's a ridiculous law. And it's an embarrassment for American citizens." Kyle McClellan, of the St. Louis Cardinals, said, "The All-Star game, it's going to generate a lot of revenue. Look at what it did here for St. Louis. It was a huge promotion for this city and this club and it's one of those things where it's something that would definitely leave a mark on them if we were to pull out of there. It would get a point across."[11]

But the biggest news was that the union, the Major League Baseball Players Association, initially spoke out. Executive director Michael Weiner issued this statement:

> The impact of the bill signed into law in Arizona last Friday is not limited to the players on one team. The international players on the [Arizona] Diamondbacks work and, with their families, reside in Arizona from April through September or October. If the current law goes into effect, the MLBPA will consider additional steps necessary to protect the rights and interests of our members.[12]

There is no record of the union's putting out a similar statement on any political issue in its history. In this flurry of comments, we saw how sports can become an electric platform for social justice. Athletes' actions and statements can humanize an issue and reach untold numbers who skip the front page and go directly to the sports section. This was one of those rare historical moments in the United States when protest helped shape athletes and, in turn, athletes helped shape the confidence, size, and scope of protest. This was seen particularly when the most famous athlete in Arizona entered the fray. He just happened to be a South African–born, Canadian-raised point guard.

"Here Come the Suns!":
The Phoenix Suns Come Out as One

While the Arizona Diamondbacks were seen as a symbol of the anti-immigrant hysteria sweeping their state, a local counterpoint emerged with the Phoenix Suns. On the Cinco de Mayo following the passage of SB 1070, the team announced that they would be wearing jerseys that read simply "Los Suns." Team owner Robert Sarver said, after talking to the team, that this would be an act of sartorial solidarity against the bill. Their opponent, the San Antonio Spurs, made clear that they supported the gesture. In fact, their coach, Gregg Popovich, said he was cross with the league because it had refused his request to wear jerseys that read "Los Spurs."[13]

In a statement released by the Suns, Sarver said, "The frustration with the federal government's failure to deal with the issue of illegal immigration resulted in passage of a flawed state law. However intended, the result . . . is that our basic principles of equal rights and protection under the law are being called into question, and Arizona's already struggling economy will suffer even further setbacks." He followed up by noting, "I looked around our plane and looked at our players and the diversity in our organization. I thought we need to go on record that we honor our diversity in our team, in the NBA, and we need to show support for that. . . . There are times you need to stand up and be heard."[14]

After Sarver spoke out, the team chimed in against the passage of SB 1070 by way of their two-time MVP point guard, Steve Nash. Nash, who in 2003 became the first athlete to go on record against the Iraq war, said, "I think the law is very misguided. I think it is unfortunately to the detriment to our society and our civil liberties and I think it is very important for us to stand up for things we believe in." All-star power forward Amar'e Stoudemire, who is now with the New York Knicks and has no political reputation, also chimed in, saying, "It's going to be great to wear Los Suns to let the Latin community know we're behind them 100%."[15]

After the story went public, I spoke on the phone with NBA Players Association president Billy Hunter about the Suns' audacious move. Hunter said,

It's phenomenal. This makes it clear to me that it's a new era. It's a new time. Athletes can tend to be apolitical and isolated from the issues that impact the general public. But now here come the Suns. I would have expected nothing less from Steve Nash, who has been out front on a number of issues over the years. I also want to recognize Amar'e. I know how strident Amar'e can be and I'm really impressed to see him channel his intensity. It shows a tremendous growth and maturity on his part. And I have to applaud Bob Sarver because he is really taking a risk by putting himself out there. I commend them. I just think it's super.

The unprecedented decision by the entire Suns organization to come out against Arizona's anti-immigrant SB 1070 inspired a sports broadcast like no other in my lifetime. It began with sideline reporter Marty Snider outside the arena covering a mushrooming three-thousand-person civil rights march, led by Reverend Al Sharpton and Phoenix mayor Phil Gordon (both wearing "Los Suns" jerseys). Then the scene switched to the pregame studio, with host Ernie Johnson and former players Kenny "the Jet" Smith, Chris Webber, and Charles Barkley. When Ernie Johnson attempted to refocus the pregame show on the game at hand, viewers got an unexpected and bracing lesson in dissent. Kenny Smith, like any good point guard, set up the others by saying, "I think it's great that the team understands, the management understands and now the people of Phoenix are all rallying together at the same time."

Barkley, a longtime Arizona resident and a man who once said that he was a Republican until "the Republicans lost their damn minds," chimed in, saying, "The only people screwing it up are the politicians. The governor—the interim governor I might add—J. D. Hayworth and John McCain . . . You know, living in Arizona for a long time, the Hispanic community, they're like the fabric of the cloth. . . . President Obama, you've got to do something because these lightweight politicians in Arizona have no idea what they are doing."

For the typically blunt Barkley to speak in such terms is hardly surprising. But it was Chris Webber who upped the ante, interrupting a visibly uncomfortable Ernie Johnson with, "Public Enemy said it a long time ago: 'By the Time I Get to Arizona.' I'm not surprised. They didn't even want there to be a Martin Luther King Day when John McCain was in [office]. So if you follow history you know that this is part of Arizona politics."

It was a remarkable display and it was difficult to not think of the millions of television viewers around the country, in sports bars, restaurants, and house parties, confronted with such forthright language. But perhaps even more important than the support Los Suns received from protesters and broadcasters was their play on the court. Phoenix trailed by nine at the end of the first quarter and Spurs star power forward Tim Duncan was scoring with ease. The crowd was dead. It wasn't difficult to envision the talk if Phoenix lost: "The political hoopla was a distraction." "This is why sports and politics don't mix." "They should have been focused on the Spurs and not immigration." Grinning smugly would have been Los Angeles Lakers coach Phil Jackson, who chided the Suns by saying, "If I heard it right the American people are really for stronger immigration laws. . . . I don't think teams should get involved in the political stuff."[16] In fact, it would have echoed Muhammad Ali's first fight with Joe Frazier, which he lost, much to the delight of all the columnists and fans who wanted to see the draft-dodging "Louisville Lip" punished by "Smokin'" Joe.

Just when we were all ready to stick a fork in the bricklaying Suns, something happened. The slick-shooting, fast-breaking team started to crash the boards, play ugly, and do all the dirty work that wins games. Doughy, undersized three-point specialist Jared Dudley started aggressively snatching offensive rebounds like his soul had been possessed by Barkley himself, energizing the crowd and shocking his team back to life. The result was a 110–102 victory in which the run-and-gun Suns were held to just eight fast-break points. Coach Alvin Gentry said afterward that he had never seen the team play with such mental toughness. The team went on to shockingly sweep the Spurs in four games. It's a toughness they took to the Lakers in the next round. Even though the Suns ultimately faltered with the Lakers, they kept the debate around SB 1070 in the public eye and further inspired those fighting to move the 2011 All-Star Game.

The Backlash

The pressure to move the game continued to be a thorn in the side of MLB commissioner Bud Selig at the start of the 2011 season. As the year opened, baseball held its annual Civil Rights Game to remember Jackie Robinson's historic breach of baseball's color line in 1947. They chose to hold the game in Georgia, where Governor Nathan Deal was on the verge of signing an SB 1070 copycat bill that promised more racial profiling and broken lives. The Georgia bill horribly echoes the days of Jim Crow, when the state's black population needed written documentation just to travel. Like Jim Crow, the bill was pushed through on racist grounds. Atlanta civil rights hero John Lewis spoke out forcefully against the legislation, saying, "This is a recipe for discrimination. We've come too far to return to the dark past."[17]

In the meantime, state senator Renee Untermann, in debating the bill, said that recent efforts at cooperation between federal immigration officials and local police were effective because she saw "fewer foreigners driving around."[18] Don't be caught "driving while brown" if Renee Unterman is in the area.

Staging the Civil Rights Game where Nathan Deal was making life hell for brown people was a tin-eared, contemptible choice. But there was Bud Selig, celebrating civil rights in Georgia while chortling about the 2011 All-Star Game in Arizona. In the hands of Selig, irony becomes arsenic. We were all lucky, however, that Selig was stupid enough to choose the Civil Rights Game to honor, among others, the great musician Carlos Santana. Santana was supposed to be the Latino stand-in, a smiling symbol of baseball's diversity—and maybe he would even play a song!

But Bud picked the wrong Latino. Carlos Santana took the microphone and said that he was representing all immigrants. Then he added, "The people of Arizona, and the people of Atlanta, Georgia, you should be ashamed of yourselves." In a perfect display of Governor Nathan Deal's Georgia, the cheers quickly turned to boos. Yes, Carlos Santana was booed on Civil Rights Game day in Atlanta for talking about civil rights.

And where was Bud Selig during all this drama? It seems that he slunk out of a stadium back door in the fifth inning.

As the year wore on, the anti-immigrant rightwing began to fear that the Arizona boycott might actually succeed and began to rally their own side. Rush Limbaugh howled for Major League Baseball to "not cave to the likes of Jesse Jackson and Al Sharpton" and move the All-Star Game out of Arizona, adding that, "The Sports World has to *man up!*" It was hardly subtle, but Limbaugh makes long green by preaching the white-power blues, so his response was hardly a surprise.

But it was not just the Limbaughs, the Becks, the Levins, and the right-wing hate machine turning up the heat. It was eminently mainstream people like CBS Sports's Gregg Doyel, who wrote,

Phoenix was once the fastest-growing big city in America. It was a place to go. Now it's a place to leave. But you're not hearing that part of the story. You're not hearing about the creeping third-world kudzu spreading into Phoenix and throughout Arizona. Nope. You're hearing about the nerve— the nerve—of lawmakers and law-enforcers in Arizona who want to get a handle on their state before it spins out of control. And so you're hearing about the role of baseball in this story. You're hearing about fans in Chicago, who are 1,804 ignorantly blissful miles from Phoenix and are boycotting the Arizona Diamondbacks when the Diamondbacks come to town to play the Cubs. . . . You're hearing that MLB should move the game, because baseball is nearly 30 percent Hispanic and out of respect to Hanley Ramirez and Albert Pujols and Alex Rodriguez, the game cannot be held in an unreasonable place that would demand that every member of its population be in this country legally. What if Miguel Cabrera is walking to the ballpark and gets deported because he doesn't have his papers?!??[19]

No mention, of course, that crime is actually down in Phoenix, or of the many other statistics that prove that these arguments rest on racism, not reality.[20] But why quibble? It's always easier to attack the immigrants.

This was the heat given off by the media about Major League Baseball's actually daring to stand for something. It was reflected on the ground in a series of rallies and speeches by politicians, Tea

Party activists, and vigilante groups like the Minutemen. Many were surprised by the anger expressed at the Diamondbacks, by the stand of Los Suns. Some called on people to root even harder for the D-backs. (Though, as one Minuteman leader said to me, "We didn't want to root against the Suns. Nash is the best player they've ever had.")

Finally, Bud Selig chose to ignore all the dissenting voices and the game went ahead as planned.

Major League Baseball has prided—and marketed—itself on historically being more than just a game. Bud Selig, in particular, publicly venerates the game's civil rights tradition. Jackie Robinson's number is retired and visible in every park, and the great Roberto Clemente has become a true baseball saint. But Selig's inaction makes his tributes to the past look as hollow as Sammy Sosa's old bat. Selig clearly loves the symbolism of civil rights more than the sacrifice.

The game, which finally took place in July 2011, meant a financial windfall for the state, as well as for Diamondbacks owner Ken Kendrick. The game also gave a national spotlight to the vile Sheriff Joe Arpaio of Arizona's Maricopa County, our twenty-first-century Bull Connor, who threatened to bring down his pink-clad chain gang to clean up outside the stadium.[21]

Unfortunately, Selig was not the only one backing down from the moment. The Major League Players Association issued a very strong statement in 2010 against SB 1070 and hinted that a boycott might be in the cards, saying they would "consider additional measures to protect the interests of our members." Then, after months of silence, Executive Director Michael Weiner said, "SB 1070 is not in effect and key portions of the law have been judged unlawful by the federal courts. Under all the circumstances, we have not asked players to refrain from participating in any All-Star activities."[22]

To say SB 1070 "is not in effect" was sophistry. Only a section

of SB 1070 has been judged unlawful: the extension of police powers to demand papers without cause. Other aspects are now on the
books, including stiffer penalties for "illegals" and giving citizens
the right to sue any city that sets up safe havens for immigrants.
In addition, Arizona governor Jan Brewer was appealing the prun-
ing of SB 1070 directly to the U.S. Supreme Court when they issued their statement. While parts of the law were struck down, the
Court eventually upheld the state's rights to do background checks
based on suspicion of being undocumented. More public dissent
may have made a difference.

My own discussions with Arizona activists reveal that racial profiling has been rampant since the law passed, with Latinos, legal
and illegal, fearful of calling the police or the fire department, or
even attending church. Even if you agree with Michael Weiner that
immigration matters "will not be resolved at Chase Field, nor on
any baseball diamond," the MLBPA was remarkably cavalier about
its responsibility to "protect its members."

The 2011 All-Star Game proceeded as planned as the players
and their union blinked. There were protests outside the stadium
but nothing inside to celebrate and build on the bravery of players and fans over the previous year. No one stormed the field. No
player wore as much as an armband. The failure to stop the game
only shows how much louder and more determined immigrants'
rights activists will have to be if they hope to be heard. For now,
baseball, with all its pretensions of its role in our civil rights narrative, has to live with the shame of standing for Arizona when it was
a pariah state.

In the end, responsibility for this debacle rests with Selig. NFL
owners, whom no one would confuse with the NAACP, threatened
to pull the 1993 Super Bowl out of Arizona if the state continued
to refuse to recognize Martin Luther King's birthday as a national
holiday. The state's voters caved. Now, twenty years later, baseball's

commissioner does nothing. Yes, Bud Selig would undoubtedly have received an avalanche of criticism if he had moved the game; that's what it means to actually sacrifice something for the sake of the civil rights he claims to hold so dear. Instead, his legacy will bear another blot, joining the steroid boom, the cancellation of the 1994 World Series, and the gouging of state economies with taxpayer-funded stadiums. Now Bud Selig can always be remembered as the Seinfeld of sports commissioners: the man who did nothing; the man who, with the game on the line, kept his bat on his shoulder and took a third strike.

· 8 ·

"Is Your Underwear
Flame Retardant?"
Sexuality and Sports

Over the last two years a very youthful, very grassroots women's movement has erupted, going by the name of SlutWalk. It began in January 2011 after a Toronto police officer told students at a campus safety information session at York University, "Women should avoid dressing like sluts in order not to be victimized." The message was that women bring sexual assault on themselves by the way they act or dress. It is a message repeated to women their entire lives, and the response in this particular case was, "Hell no." A march was called. Posters were put up around campus that listed York University "don'ts"—including entries like "Don't go to pub night" and "Don't worry your pretty little head. Don't think too much. Don't get mad and definitely . . . Don't organize!" They couldn't have known, but they had just started a new movement.[1]

In boisterous demonstrations around the country—and the world—SlutWalk has aimed to smash the age-old idea that women cannot be three-dimensional, sexual human beings. It's a movement against objectification and degradation. It's a movement that calls for a loud rejection of sexist stereotypes and demands sexual freedom for all women. It's a movement against men setting the terms for how women see their bodies, their minds, and their potential. And it's a movement that is very much needed in the world of sports. Look no further than two of the most high-profile female athletes in the country: Danica Patrick and Candace Parker.

In 2008, Danica Patrick accomplished two firsts: she became both the first woman to win an Indy car race and the first race car driver to appear in the men's magazine *FHM.* In *FHM,* Patrick was clad in red leather underwear, with her legs spread on the hood of a car. The pictures were accompanied by a short interview where Patrick answered questions like "Is your underwear flame retardant?" and "Are there times of the month when you are a more aggressive or angry driver?"[2]

Candace Parker also has a cover to her name—one that couldn't contrast more sharply with Patrick's. Parker is arguably the greatest women's basketball player in the world. She will dunk on your head. She also spent a good part of 2009 pregnant. *ESPN The Magazine* put Parker on their cover in glowing maternal white, cradling her belly. The article opens with lavish praise: "Candace Parker is beautiful. Breathtaking, really, with flawless skin, endless legs and a C cup. . . . She is a woman who plays like a man, one of the boys, if the boys had C cups and flawless skin and perfect, white teeth." The article then brings Danica Patrick into the discussion, noting that "Patrick is nowhere near the best in her field, but she doesn't need to be, because she is hot enough to pose for *Maxim.* While that works for her, Parker wants more."[3]

First of all, one can only imagine how people would respond to an article about Denver Broncos quarterback Peyton Manning that started, "Peyton Manning is handsome. Breathtaking, really, with flawless skin, endless legs and a medium jock strap he shows off at every turn."

Comparisons aside, though, the entire Danica Patrick–and–Candace Parker dynamic here is frustrating, angering, even infuriating. Most of all, it is very tired. Women athletes have been trapped in the same box for a century. This trap dictates that women must be girls first, athletes second. And, most critically, women athletes must shout at the tops of their lungs that they are absolutely hetero, so straight that their dreams include having pregnant bellies or being on a magazine passed around a frat house.

Mary Jo Kane, a sociologist from the University of Minnesota who specializes in gender and sports, undertook a far-reaching study to understand the effect of sexualizing women athletes. When Kane and her research team showed images of female athletes displaying their bodies to a diverse focus group of both men and women, they found a very basic truth: sex may sell magazines, but it doesn't sell women's sports. As Kane said to me in an interview, "It alienates the core of the fan base that's already there. Women . . . eighteen to thirty-four and thirty-five to fifty-five are offended by these images. And older males, fathers with daughters, taking their daughters to sporting events to see their favorite female athletes, are deeply offended by these images." As for the young men excited to see Danica Patrick in leather, spread out on a car, "they want to buy the magazines but they didn't want to consume the sports."

This ought to be an earth-shaking revelation for every executive in the Women's Tennis Association, the WNBA, and the LPGA, who have for decades operated under the assumption that a little leg goes a long way. But women's sports, Kane argues, will need more than logic to move away from the abyss of abject objectification: "This is deeper. This is also about what runs in the bone marrow of women's sports, namely homophobia." In other words, sports leagues take as a given that people see women athletes as some 1970s stereotype of a "butch lesbian," so they try to push women athletes about as far from that as possible. If that takes a thong, then so be it.

But to what extent are female athletes themselves at fault? What about those who say that provocative poses are about celebrating their bodies, and that celebration of the "body beautiful" has been a part of sports since ancient Greece? Kane answers, "What muscle group do bare breasts belong to? You can show off your body without being naked in a passive, sexually provocative pose."

This question of breasts as a "muscle group" is about more than whether women's sports is taking itself seriously. It points to whether universities, boosters, and donors take it seriously, as well. And it is, Kane believes, about the future of college athletics, because "the end result of this is that when resources are precious, and you dole out those resources, and you don't take women's athletics as seriously as men's, then there are tangible consequences. Athletic directors get a pass to just not take it seriously."

The Vise

The vise for women athletes is always and forever present: sexism on one side, homophobia on the other. This vise is what crushed an eighteen-year-old South African runner by the name of Caster Semenya.

Caster set a world record in the eight-hundred-meter sprint at the 2009 African Junior Championships. She should be training for the Olympics; instead she spent time on suicide watch. This has everything to do with the twisted way track and field—and the sports world at large—understands gender.

The more Caster won, the more she shaved seconds off her personal bests, the more her drug tests came back negative, the more her competitors whispered: Her muscles don't look like a woman's.

Her hips don't look like a woman's. Her voice doesn't sound like a woman's. She's too fast! Too good! In the culture of women's track and field, there could only be one conclusion: someone this good must be "part man."

The rumors spread, pressure mounted, and international track and field officials proceeded to subject Caster to "gender testing," which included invasive examinations of the eighteen-year-old by a gynecologist, an endocrinologist, and a psychologist. Then, the humiliation: test results were leaked to the press, claiming to show that she has internal testes and no womb or ovaries. (It should be noted that the actual, official test results have never been made public and were deemed confidential.)[4]

It's possible that Caster Semenya is one of the millions of people in the world (one of 1,666 births per year in the United States alone) who are classified as "intersex."[5] Or she may have AIS, androgen insensitivity syndrome, which affects as many as five out of one hundred thousand births.[6] Whatever Caster Semenya's biological makeup, it should be a private issue between her and her doctor—and it certainly shouldn't prevent her from competing or be grounds for derision. Instead, Semenya became a punch line. A news segment about her on MSNBC was preceded by the Aerosmith song "Dude Looks Like a Lady."

What these officials still don't understand, or confront, is that gender—that is, how we comport and conceive of ourselves—is a remarkably fluid social construction. Even our physical sex is far more ambiguous than is often imagined or taught. Medical science has long acknowledged the existence of millions of people whose bodies combine anatomical features that are conventionally associated with either men or women and/or have chromosomal variations of XX or XY. Many of these "intersex" individuals are legally operated on by surgeons who force traditional norms of genitalia onto newborn infants. In what some doctors consider a "psychosocial emergency," thousands of healthy babies are effectively subject to clitoridectomy if a clitoris is "too large" or castration if a penis is "too small" (evidently penises are never considered "too big").[7]

Track and field has had a particular preoccupation with gender, especially when it intersects with race. Fifty years ago, Olympic official Norman Cox proposed that the International Olympic Committee create a separate category of competition for black women, "the unfairly advantaged 'hermaphrodites.'" For years, women athletes had to parade naked in front of Olympic officials for inspection. This gave way to more "sophisticated gender testing" to determine if athletes have what officials still perceive as the ultimate advantage: being a man.

Let's leave aside that being male is not the be-all, end-all of athletic success; wealth, coaching facilities, nutrition, and opportunity determine the development of a world-class athlete far more than a Y chromosome ever could. Essentially, the physical reality of intersex people calls into question fixed notions we are taught to accept about men and women in general, and athletes in sex-segregated sports like track and field in particular. While we are never encouraged to conceive of biology in this way, male and female bodies are more similar than they are distinguishable from each other. And when training and nutrition are equal, it is increasingly difficult to tell the difference (picture, for example, the top male and female Olympic swimmers wearing state-of-the-art one-piece speed suits). Title IX, the 1972 law that imposed equal funding for girls' and boys' sports in schools, has radically altered not only women's fitness and emotional well-being but their bodies as well.

In the Caster Semenya case, there are important questions few in the sports media dared ask. Why should it matter if she is maxing out her every biological advantage? No one claims that basketball star Yao Ming had an unfair advantage because he is seven foot five. No one asked if swimmer Michael Phelps's mammoth, flipper-like feet unfairly skewed the competition. If anything, he was praised for being, as one announcer said breathlessly, "built to swim!" Why isn't Caster Semenya, with her slender hips and powerful muscles, "built to run"? If Semenya's biology is not "normal," it's worth asking, what world-class athlete does have a normal body? As Tommy Craggs of Deadspin wrote,

> Great athletes tend not to come from the vast middle of human life. They're all freaks in one way or another. . . . But Semenya has nevertheless been portrayed as some lone oddity on the margins, like some Elephant Man of sports, with everyone obsessing like Victorian scientists over the presence of a couple internal testicles. It's funny: People seem to think her very weirdness is grounds enough for stripping her of her medal and drumming her out of track. But this is sports. Her weirdness is perfectly normal.[8]

Clearly, it's the "her" that gets Semenya in trouble. Exceptional male athletes are treated like kings, not sideshow freaks. But for women to join them on the royal dais, they must appear as if they can step seamlessly from the court or track and into the pages of soft-core porn. Freaks need not apply.

The Western media's handling of the Caster Semenya story was at best simplistic and at worst repellent. On various radio shows, it was asked, "Why does she talk like a man?" and "Do you think she's really a dude? Is this a *Crying Game* thing?" Most of these questions reveal more about the questioners' insecurities than about Semenya's situation. The derision was not limited to the confines of sports radio. I appeared on Campbell Brown's now-defunct CNN show, where my co-panelist, Dr. Jennifer Berman, said that suspicion of Semenya's gender was justified because she is "eight feet tall." Caster is five foot seven—and this is hysteria, pure and simple, born out of people's own discomfort with women athletes who don't conform to gender stereotypes.

In South Africa, however, the response could not have been more different. Semenya was greeted by thousands of people in a celebration that included signs and songs from the antiapartheid struggle. She was even embraced by former South African first lady Winnie Mandela. "We are here to tell the whole world how proud we are of our little girl," Mandela told cheering fans. "They can write what they like—we are proud of her."[9]

As Patrick Bond, a leading South African global justice activist, said to me,

> To order Semenya tested for gender seems about as reasonable as ordering International Association of Athletics Federations officials like Philip Weiss tested for brain cells—which actually isn't a bad idea given his recent off-field performance. And if Weiss doesn't have a sufficient number of brain cells to know how to treat women athletes, it would only be fair to relieve him of his functions for the good of world athletics.

It's not just national political figures with global profiles who are embracing Semenya. The people have rallied around her fiercely, particularly in the rural, impoverished, subsistence-farming community where Semenya was raised. Her home village, Ga-Masehlong, has an unemployment rate near 80 percent; they only recently acquired electricity. As *The Guardian* wrote:

> The loyalty of Semenya's friends and neighbours is striking. South Africa's rural communities are typically regarded as bastions of social conservatism divided into traditional gender roles and expectations of femininity. But there is no evidence that Semenya, an androgynous tomboy who played football

and wore trousers, was ostracised by her peers. Instead, they are shocked at what they perceive as the intolerance and prurience of western commentators.

"They are jealous," said Dorcus Semenya, the athlete's mother, who led villagers in jubilant singing and dancing upon Caster's return. "I say to them, go to hell, you don't know what you're saying. They're jealous because they don't want black people improving their status."[10]

It perhaps shouldn't be so surprising that Caster's neighbors recognize the West's "intolerance and prurience." Unlike the United States, South Africa has legalized same-sex marriage, and unlike the United States, South Africa legally prohibits discrimination based on sexuality. By no means is South Africa some sort of LGBT Shangri-la. But this does suggest that the United States could stand to learn a thing or two about discrimination and human sexuality.

There is currently no definitive information regarding Semenya's sexual orientation or gender choice. We should use this opportunity to continue debating the pros and cons of gender segregation in sports, but we must abandon the ludicrous terms that have so far framed this case for a conversation that acknowledges the fluidity of gender in sports and beyond. At this point, all we know for sure is that Semenya identifies herself as an eighteen-year-old woman—and that she can run like the wind.

What is the solution, then, for how the International Olympic Committee should deal with this? Scholars Rebecca Jordan-Young and Katrina Karzakis laid out a lucid plan in the *New York Times*. As they wrote:

First, at the very least, female athletes should be allowed to compete throughout any investigation. Suspending them from competition once questions are raised violates their confidentiality and imposes sanctions before relevant information has been gathered.

Second, when it comes to sex, sports authorities should acknowledge that while science can offer evidence, it cannot dictate what evidence we should use. . . .

Testosterone is one of the most slippery markers that sports authorities have come up with yet. Yes, average testosterone levels are markedly different for men and women. But levels vary widely depending on time of day, time of life, social status and—crucially—one's history of athletic training. . . .

Third, if we want a clear answer to who is eligible for women's competitions, it is time to stop pawning this fundamentally social question off onto scientists. . . .

Fourth, any policies must be developed through a transparent process with broad input. . . .

Finally, the I.O.C. and other sports governing bodies should denounce gender bashing among athletes, coaches, the news media and fans. Policing women's testosterone would exacerbate one of the ugliest tendencies in women's sports today: the name-calling and the insinuations that an athlete is "too masculine," or worse, that she is a man.[11]

Unfortunately for women athletes, you can't be too tough for fear you'll be called a lesbian. You can't be too aggressive for fear that you will be called mannish. You must be an outdated stereotype of a woman before you are an athlete. These suffocating norms have held for more than a century.

The Babe

Mildred Ella "Babe" Didrikson was the most famous female athlete of the first half of the twentieth century. She won three medals in track and field in the 1932 Olympics and later became the standard for all women golfers. Yet despite her towering athletic accomplishments, Didrikson was denounced as "mannish" and "not-quite female," a "Muscle Moll" who could not "compete with other girls in the very ancient and time honored sport of mantrapping."[12]

Hearing that, in addition to track and field, she also played basketball, football, and numerous other sports, an astonished journalist once asked Didrikson, "Is there anything you don't play?" Without missing a beat, she reportedly answered, "Yeah, dolls."[13]

Didrikson then disappeared and returned in the 1950s, donning long hair, wearing a ton of makeup, and playing golf, which was considered a woman's sport. She also resurfaced married to a mammoth pro wrestler named George Zaharias. Sportswriters loved it, gleefully writing, "Along came a great big he-man and the Babe forgot all her man-hating chatter." One headline read, "Babe Is a Lady Now: The World's Most Amazing Athlete Has Learned to Wear Nylons and Cook for Her Huge Husband."

Why have we covered such a short distance over so many years? Why is there so much sexism and homophobia in sports, even in the twenty-first century? The reasons derive from the ways that formal sports—as apart from informal play—were first promoted in the United States.

Organized sports did not emerge in this country until the end of the nineteenth century. At that time, most women were denied participation, which also meant they were denied access to exercise, a unique form of camaraderie, and the mental training believed necessary to lead the much-heralded New American Century.

In the early 1900s, some wealthy women started to gain access to the country club sports of golf and tennis—but these offered no refuge. Tennis, in particular, was more pain than pleasure. At the time, women were forced to play in corsets so constricting that they would cause the wearers to pass out.

When early women's rights activists began to demand equal

access to sports, a cottage industry of quack science developed explaining how sports would cause infertility, nymphomania, everything short of growing a tail. One writer in an 1878 edition of the *American Christian Review* diagrammed the twelve-step downfall of any woman who dared engage in the sinful world of croquet. It is truly a slippery slope:

1. Social party.
2. Social and play party.
3. Croquet party.
4. Picnic and croquet party.
5. Picnic, croquet and dance.
6. Absence from church.
7. Immoral conduct.
8. Exclusion from the church.
9. A runaway match [more croquet].
10. Poverty.
11. Shame and disgrace.
12. Ruin.

The age of the whalebone corset started to crack in part due to the invention of the bicycle. Alarmed, the science community rose up again, proving conclusively that riding a bicycle could implode the uterus. Doctors also claimed that women would be susceptible to what they called the "bicycle face," a condition where excessive riding would leave a permanent scowl consisting of a "protruding jaw, wild staring eyes, and strained expression."[14]

For women activists, access to physical play came to symbolize their very liberation. Pioneering feminist Elizabeth Cady Stanton, in a piece for the women's magazine *The Lily*, wholeheartedly rejected claims of a man's "physical superiority," writing, "We cannot say what the woman might be physically, if the girl were allowed all the freedom of the boy, in romping, swimming, climbing, or playing ball." Cady Stanton's argument—that nurture, not nature, determines a man's physical and sporting superiority—was a gutsy one. But it was an argument she and other activists lost: by the 1900s, women had narrowly won the right to play, but in separate and unequal facilities.

Indeed, the first generation of women's gym teachers claimed that sports had to be segregated by gender because only under their watchful eyes could women be prevented from "loss of sexual control" and "emotional stimulation." These teachers were also positioned as the guardians against the dangers of lesbianism as an outgrowth of play. As Susan K. Cahn wrote in *Coming On Strong,* one PE director promised that women's sports would not create "the loud masculinely dressed man-aping individual but the whole hearted rosy cheeked healthy girl."[15]

Yet in these early days, every time a woman showed that she could compete, she excelled. In 1922, Sybil Bauer set the world record in the backstroke, beating the men's record. Then Gertrude Ederle swam the English Channel two hours faster than any man. When Ederle set that record, newspapers said with great trepidation that it was "a battle won for feminism."[16]

But as new sports opened up to women, old stereotypes held them back. The Amateur Athletic Union would integrate beauty pageants into the big athletic tourneys. It was common for PE programs to require that PE majors "have or possess the possibilities of an attractive personal appearance."[17]

This backlash—and the country—got turned on its head during World War II. Just as Rosie the Riveter symbolized a massive shift in the area of work, the All-American Girls Professional Baseball League (AAGPBL) became a symbol of transformation in the world of sports. The league, immortalized in the movie *A League of Their Own*, popularized women's professional baseball in many parts of the country from 1943 to 1955.

There was much to celebrate in the AAGPBL—the fact that women were playing hardball and not softball, the high level of play, and the support it received (at its height, the league drew one million fans in a year). But the players had to wear skirts and follow what management called a "femininity principle," which meant makeup, long hair, and a mandatory evening charm school. Any hint of lesbianism meant prompt dismissal; Josephine D'Angelo, for example, was released immediately after getting a bob haircut.[18]

The AAGPBL was taken apart after the end of the war, when the country set about ushering Rosie the Riveter out of the factory and back to the kitchen and making babies. June Cleaver was the new ideal, and women were whole only in the home. This era was also characterized by McCarthyite raids against LGBT people, mass firings of suspected homosexuals from government jobs, and attacks on gay bars. In turn, virulent homophobia assaulted women's sports in the 1950s, far more explicitly than in the past.

What had previously been coded as fear of the "mannish" athlete or queers now was naked homophobia. At the national 1956 conference of collegiate women physical educators, the guest speaker, Dr. Josephine Renshaw, gave a talk with the benign title of "Activities for Mature Living." The rant warned against the "muscular Amazon with unkempt hair, clod hopper shoes, and dowdy clothing who would become disappointed in heterosexual attachments and see women's sports in a predatory fashion."[19]

This was the terrain upon which women competed (or not) until the late 1960s, when a growing women's movement made demands for equality in society and the world of sports alike. This manifested itself most clearly in the passage of Title IX—the 1972 law stipulating that "no person in the United States shall, on the basis of sex, be excluded from participation in, be denied the benefits of, or be subjected to discrimination under any education program or activity receiving Federal financial assistance"—and the emergence of the great Billie Jean King.

The new movement roared to a big victory when Billie Jean King faced off against Bobby Riggs in their "Battle of the Sexes" tennis match, called by the London *Sunday Times* "the drop shot and volley heard around the world." Riggs, a 1939 Wimbledon champion, had already swept the court with women's champion Margaret Court on Mother's Day in 1973. King, who previously had rejected Riggs's dare to play, accepted his latest challenge. "I thought it would set us back 50 years if I didn't win that match," the twelve-time Grand Slam winner said. "It would ruin the women's tour and affect all women's self-esteem."[20]

The "Battle of the Sexes" captured the entire country's imagination. On September 20, 1973, in Houston, King was carried out on the Astrodome court like Cleopatra, in a gold throne held aloft by four muscular men dressed as ancient slaves. Riggs was wheeled in on a rickshaw pulled by models in tight outfits who were referred to as "Bobby's Bosom Buddies."

Their entrances turned out to be the most competitive part of the day, as King, then twenty-nine, ran Riggs ragged, winning 6–4, 6–3, 6–3. As Neil Amdur wrote in the *New York Times,* "Most important perhaps for women everywhere, she convinced skeptics that a female athlete can survive pressure-filled situations and that men are as susceptible to nerves as women." The great Frank Deford wrote in *Sports Illustrated,* "She has prominently affected the way 50 percent of society thinks and feels about itself in the vast area of physical exercise." He continued, "Moreover, like [Arnold] Palmer, she has made a whole sports boom because of the singular force of her presence."[21]

King was far more than an athlete or a symbol. She was an

activist for women's equal rights. In the words of Navratilova, she "embodied the crusader fighting a battle for all of us. She was carrying the flag; it was all right to be a jock."[22] King, who had received $15,000 less than Ilie Nastase did for winning the U.S. Open in 1972, called for a strike by women's players if the prize money wasn't equal by the following year. In 1973, the U.S. Open became the first major tournament to offer an equal winner's purse for men and women. King also fought for a women's players' union and forged the Women's Tennis Association, which elected her its first president in 1973.

It was for her role in the movements of the day that *Life* magazine named her one of the "100 most important Americans of the 20th century." King was the only female athlete on the list, and one of only four athletes. Of the other three, two—Jackie Robinson and Muhammad Ali—are also strongly associated with social movements (Babe Ruth was the third).

As for Title IX, today one in three young girls plays sports; forty years ago, that number was one in thirty-four. Young women who play sports are less likely to suffer from osteoporosis, eating disorders, and depression, among other things. This law has improved the quality of life for tens of millions of women across the country.[23]

The LGBT Landscape

For pro women athletes, sports remains largely a place of denigration, not celebration. Swimsuit issues, cheerleaders, and beer-commercial sexism frame women all too narrowly in a testosterone-addled sports world. Unsurprisingly, homophobia is still a major issue. While some prominent women athletes, like the great basketball player Sheryl Swoopes, have come out of the closet, you can count the number on one hand.

The idea that athletes will routinely come out of the closet in the absence of a broader movement challenging homophobia is pure fantasy. This is why the few challenges to the homophobic status quo in sports must be highlighted and brought out of the "media closet." Take the case of Jen Harris. Jen was one of the leading scorers for the Penn State women's basketball team and a WNBA prospect. Then she was suddenly cut from the team. Jen is a lesbian. And her coach, Rene Portland, a two-time coach of the year whose nickname was "Mom," had three rules: no drugs, no drinking, and no lesbians.[24]

Jen refused to take it and sued for discrimination. Students rallied in support, and soon other Penn State players came forward, revealing a twenty-seven-year history of psychological abuse, humiliation, and discrimination. It's because of the Rene Portlands that Caster Semenya had to be put on suicide watch. It's because of the Rene Portlands that we need a movement for sexual liberation that frames access to athletics as a right and not a privilege. And it's because of brave athletes like Jen Harris that we have a road map of how to fight this level of discrimination in women's sports.

Now, what about the boys? I don't want to shock anybody, but being gay in a men's locker room is not exactly easy. It's difficult to imagine a more oppressive atmosphere. In the world of pro sports, antigay slurs can seem as ingrained as racism was fifty years ago. To be gay is to be weak. To be gay is to be vulnerable. To accept gay teammates is also to accept that all that butt slapping, roughhousing, and co-showering could have other meanings.

Beyond the slurs that have become part of their everyday slang ("That's a nice shirt . . . no homo"), athletes blithely get away with brazenly homophobic comments. Jeremy Shockey, the gimpy part-time Saints tight end (and full-time jackass), called Coach Bill Parcells a "homo" and said he "wouldn't stand" for a gay teammate. John Smoltz, the pitcher whose two favorite movies (seriously) are

The Passion of the Christ and *Dumb and Dumber,* volunteered his views on gay marriage (he wasn't asked): "What's next? Marrying animals?"[25]

Players like Mets future Hall of Fame catcher Mike Piazza and Jeff Garcia have felt the need to hold press conferences just to tell the world that they are not gay. Then you have the Evangelical Christian organization Athletes in Action, with connections to groups that promote reparative therapy for gays and lesbians, that is a presence in many locker rooms.

As of today, no active player in the Big Three men's sports—baseball, basketball, and football—has come out of the closet. It's no wonder why, as players would risk financial, if not physical, ruin in doing so. This is why the athletes who have come out of the closet have left it until after they retired. Esera Tuaolo, Dave Kopay, and Ron Simmons of the NFL; John Amaechi of the NBA; and Billy Bean in Major League Baseball all took this route.

One important exception to this history can be found in the late Glenn Burke. While no male athlete in the United States has ever come out as an active player, we should remember Burke as a player who was out to his teammates, if not the public, thirty-five years ago. Burke is the answer to multiple trivia questions: Who was the only rookie to start in the 1977 World Series? Who invented the high five? And who was the first gay Major League baseball player—to our knowledge—to be out of the closet in the presence of his teammates, if not the fans? But Burke's story is as important as it is unknown. He was an Oakland legend, playing both baseball and hoops with pro potential. He was also a young man, growing up in the Bay Area, confident about his sexuality. That confidence, for anyone, was rare back then, but to find it in a male star athlete is remarkable. His confidence was put to the test when he made the big leagues. Dodgers teammates like Dusty Baker, Davey Lopes, Reggie Smith, Rick Monday, and Manny Mota tell the story of a player whose sexuality was noticed, recognized, and even accepted by some teammates but looked on with horror by management. After all, when you wear a red jockstrap in the locker room, people start to talk. The Dodgers organization even offered Burke $75,000 to get married, which is particularly gobsmacking.

Later, when Burke was traded to Oakland, the pressures intensified. Former teammate Claudell Washington tells this anecdote in the brilliant documentary *Out: The Glenn Burke Story*: "[A's manager Billy Martin] was introducing all the [new] players and then he got to Glenn and said, 'Oh, by the way, this is Glenn Burke and he's a faggot.'" By 1980, Burke was out of the game, but the story doesn't end there. *Out* then tells the story of Burke's life after baseball: triumphantly coming out to *Sport* magazine and Bryant Gumbel on the *Today* show, participating in the first Gay Games in 1982, and being a public figure in San Francisco. Burke's life then took a tragic turn as drugs, petty crime, and the AIDS epidemic claimed his life. He died in 1995 at the too-young age of forty-two.

The grand unanswered question in Burke's story is: how good could he have been without the relentless pressures of homophobia? To hear Dusty Baker tell it, he could have been one of the greats. Today there is a movement to enshrine Glenn Burke in the Baseball Hall of Fame and recognize him as the trailblazer he is. Given that baseball has the only Hall of Fame that explicitly says that they factor in off-field contributions, his enshrinement would be very appropriate.

But Burke's life raises another, very obvious question: why can the locker room be such an unforgiving place? There is a real material reason why men's sports is so homophobic. It's been built into organized sports in the United States from the very beginning. And to understand the roots of homophobia in sports, we have to know our history and look at the foundations of men's sports in our society.

After the Civil War, there was a period of rampant industrial

development, expansion, and immigration. The numbers are stag-
gering. From 1860 to 1900, the population of the United States
grew from 31 to 75 million. Railroads were built that spanned the
country. This was an era of booms for the new rich—robber barons
like Rockefeller, Vanderbilt, and Carnegie—and busts for everyone
else.[26]

In 1877, as the economy tanked, the reasons for unrest mul-
tiplied. Clearly, young immigrant boys needed to be given more
than a sweatshop job or a street corner. Robber barons started to
invest millions of dollars to make sure sports were an option for
this potentially volatile population. They funded and launched the
Young Men's Christian Association, or YMCA, about which one
historian wrote, "The Y's gospel was play was no longer a sin but a
way to glory God . . . and Jesus was now a stud."[27] By 1880, there
were 261 Y's scattered across the U.S. Rockefeller, Carnegie, and
Vanderbilt then took a step further and underwrote the first Public
Schools Athletic League, which funded sports in urban schools for
the first time.

But the sports explosion wasn't just about controlling immigrants and the poor. It was also about shaping young members of
the elite class so they would be fit to rule. The robber barons understandably feared that their own pampered, privileged children
would be completely unprepared to navigate the violent world they
had helped to create. Their concern bordered on the hysterical. As
Oliver Wendell Holmes wrote in the *Atlantic Monthly* in the mid-
nineteenth century, "I am satisfied that such a set of black-coated,
stiff-jointed, soft-muscled, paste-complexioned youth as we can
boast in our Atlantic cities never before sprang from the loins of
Anglo-Saxon lineage."[28] (I don't think anyone regrets that "sprang
from the loins" has left the language.)

Sports were seen as the answer for these stiff-jointed folks, and
a word was actually created for those who didn't like sports: "sissy."

Elite schools such as Harvard, Yale, and Brown launched intercollegiate football, which came to resemble something out of *Braveheart,* with students literally dying on the field.

If we take a step back, we can discern why today's sports world can be so twisted about masculinity. The heart of the founding of modern athletics was economic elites sending their children to die in Ivy League football games merely because they were terrified that they wouldn't be tough enough to lead conquests abroad and industrial brutality at home. And failure to do so made you a "sissy."

This culture of death was proudly known as Muscular Christianity. Its most prominent spokesperson was an aristocratic boxer named Theodore Roosevelt. Railing repeatedly against sissies everywhere, Roosevelt saw tough athletic training as a way to build the basis for a new American Century.

This can all seem like macho idiocy—and some of it is. But it was not all machismo for machismo's sake. Ideas like Muscular Christianity were about preparing the United States for empire. During this period, the U.S. set out to invade the Philippines, Latin America, and the Caribbean; the value of sports was deeply tied to imperialist notions of conquest and missionary zeal. Albert Spalding (of Spalding sporting goods) spoke proudly about baseball as a kind of helping hand for U.S. empire, writing,

> Baseball has proudly "followed the flag.". . . . It has followed the flag to the Hawaiian Islands, and at once supplanted every other form of athletics. It has followed the flag to the Philippines, to Puerto Rico, and to Cuba, and wherever a ship floating the stars and stripes finds anchorage today, somewhere on a nearby shore the American national game is in progress.[29]

The U.S. athlete became the embodiment not only of manliness, but of something akin to Conan the Barbarian. It is partly for this

reason that there is so much homophobia in sports: it has always
been about selling a supremely militaristic, dominant image of the
United States back to ourselves. After all, who tossed the coin at
the 2009 Super Bowl? It wasn't John Elway or Joe Montana. It was
General David Petraeus.

But this militarized, homophobic code of athletics has been
challenged again and again.

Tom Waddell, a decathlete at the 1968 Olympics, came out of
the closet, got political, and started what he first called the Gay
Olympics in San Francisco in 1982. The idea was that they would
be open to everyone, regardless of skill and, of course, sexual orientation. This was very daring, and it offended all the right people. The International Olympic Committee (IOC) and the United
States Olympic Committee (USOC) sued Waddell and the other
organizers to prevent them from using the word "Olympics." They
would be the Gay Games. This was the first time the IOC had ever
sued for the usage of a word that had been brandished by organizations ranging from the Special Olympics to the Nebraska Rat
Olympics. But Waddell wouldn't quit. He also crafted a very different vision of what sports could be. In outlining his mission early
in the process, Waddell said, "The Gay Games are not separatist,
they are not exclusive, they are not oriented to victory, they are not
for commercial gain. They're intended to bring a global community
together in friendship, to elevate consciousness and self-esteem."[30]

The opening ceremonies at the first Gay Olympics were led not
by a four-star general but by Tina Turner.

In 1986, even though the IOC held a lien on Tom Waddell's
house as part of their lawsuits, the games went on as scheduled.
They tripled in size, with three thousand athletes attending from
eighteen countries to compete in seventeen different sports. There
were three times as many women as men in the 1986 power-lifting
events. And openly HIV-positive people competed, at a time when

the disease was ignored by the Reagan administration and known in great swaths of the country as "the gay plague." Sean O'Neil, a tennis player from San Francisco, said, "I'm playing for all the other people with AIDS."[31]

The 1994 Gay Games IV were held in New York City, this time attracting more than eleven thousand participants in thirty-one events as the largest athletic competition in history. Prior to the games, a political campaign had pushed the Clinton administration to allow HIV-positive individuals from outside the United States to enter the country without special permits to attend the event. That was the first time that was ever allowed. Greg Louganis, a four-time Olympic gold medalist in diving who became HIV-positive, came out at the Gay Games.

While the Gay Games are inspiring for those of us who want to see a level playing field, today there is an even greater reason to be positive. What started with individual acts of resistance has become a broad movement for LBGT rights. And this movement is starting to find voice in the world of sports. In 2009, Baltimore Ravens linebacker and two-time Pro Bowler Brendon Ayanbadejo came out for full marriage equality, saying, "We will look back in 10, 20, 30 years and be amazed that gays and lesbians did not have the same rights as everyone else."[32] Then Saints linebacker Scott Fujita endorsed the October 2009 National Equality March, saying of Brendan Ayanbadejo's remarks,

I hope he's right in his prediction, and I hope even more that it doesn't take that long. People could look at this issue without blinders on . . . the blinders imposed by their church, their parents, their friends, or in our case, their coaches and locker rooms. I wish they would realize that it's not a religion issue. It's not a government issue. It's not even a gay/straight issue or a question of your manhood. It's a human issue.[33]

At the 2010 Super Bowl, Fujita took advantage of the media spot-light to speak out for LGBT rights, and his story was picked up by the *New York Times,* the *Boston Globe,* and many other publications. When football players—the ultimate embodiment of Muscular Christianity—speak out, they actively challenge a backward and divisive idea about what it means to be a "real man." That is something we should celebrate.

And many fans do. In a poll published by *Sports Illustrated* in 2005, an astounding 86 percent of fans said that it's "O.K. for male athletes to participate in sports, even if they are openly gay."[34]

There are other reasons to celebrate. As activist Sherry Wolf notes,

> With a stunning 80 percent support, NHL players are practically ready to host Lady Gaga on their Gay Pride float, per-haps reflecting the abundance of players from gay-friendlier Canada. In fact, Blackhawks defenseman Brent Sopel accepted an invitation from the Chicago Gay Hockey Association to stand atop its float alongside his team's Stanley Cup trophy at the 2010 Gay Pride parade. Even 57 percent of NFL players, emblems of the most orthodox hyper-masculinity, say they would play with an openly gay teammate, despite buga-boos about the locker-room showers.[35]

Unfortunately, the media tends to focus on the crassly bigoted statements of players like former NBA all-star Tim Hardaway, who said, "I hate gay people," in response to the 2007 coming-out story of retired NBA player John Amaechi. There was far less publicity when Hardaway later traveled to El Paso, Texas, where he went to college, to stand up for gay rights. A group in El Paso was trying to recall mayor John Cook and two members of the city council for re-establishing domestic-partner benefits for both gay and unmarried couples. Hardaway arrived from Miami to speak at a press conference organized by the No Recall group. "It's not right to not let the gays and lesbians have equal rights here," Hardaway told the crowd. "If I know El Paso, like they came together when the 1966 team won a championship and Don Haskins started those five [black] guys, I know the city will grow and understand that gays and lesbians need equal rights."[36]

Hardaway was referencing UTEP's 1966 national championship, when coach Don Haskins's all-black starting five made history by beating Adolph Rupp's all-white Kentucky squad. Maybe Hardaway came to understand that his earlier position also ran against the currents of change. "My family and friends came to me and were like, 'What are you doing?'" he said. "I talked to them and they made me understand that wasn't right." Amaechi, for one, is understandably skeptical about Hardaway's change of heart, saying, "I hope this is a story of true redemption rather than a savvy p.r. ploy." He added, "Either way, he is at least saying the right words, and that will make a positive difference."

The New "F-Word"

Positive steps aside, there is still a ways to go—and more and more, the struggle for LGBT rights is being fully articulated in the world of sports. On the same day in May 2011 when Chicago Bulls center Joakim Noah was fined for using a homophobic slur against a fan, a commercial for LGBT marriage rights was released featuring Suns all-star Steve Nash. The previous month, the same day Kobe Bryant was caught on camera using the same invective against a referee, Phoenix Suns players Grant Hill and Jared Dudley were filming a public service announcement where they spoke out against using the word "gay" to mean stupid, dumb, or worthy of disrespect.

That May, Suns executive Rick Welts made history when he became the highest-ranking executive to ever come out of the closet.

When the most famous Phoenix Sun ever, Charles Barkley, spoke at length in support of Welts, the media obsessed over his comments that he had gay teammates. His retort was sharp: "It bothers me when I hear these reporters and jocks get on TV and say: 'Oh, no guy can come out in a team sport. These guys would go crazy.' First of all, quit telling me what I think. I'd rather have a gay guy who can play than a straight guy who can't play."[37]

There are only two possible conclusions we can draw from this unprecedented collision between the NBA and the politics of LGBT rights. The first is that the Phoenix Suns organization must be the most gay-friendly workplace on earth, festooned with rainbows and good vibes. The other is that while homophobic outbursts are still very much a part of the vocabulary of professional sports, more and more players are calling them out as unacceptable. It was beautifully bracing to hear ESPN announcer Mark Jackson legitimately upset when he heard that Noah's fine was $50,000, only half of Kobe Bryant's fine. "That is a human being [Noah] said that to. You don't speak that way to another human being. Why the double standard?"[38]

The fact that it's Joakim Noah, of all players, who was caught on camera is in and of itself illustrative. Noah spoke out against the war in Iraq. He's called for college players to be paid by the NCAA. He put his name to a statement in defense of the Jena Six (African American teenagers facing decades in prison for a schoolyard fight). I met Noah, and he came across as one of the good guys—a true Jock for Justice. If he would drop an "F-bomb" in the heat of a game, it really says something about how ingrained it is in the language of pro competition (or that, like many of us outside of sports, Noah is progressive on some issues but not others).

But history shows that change will come. I recently had the privilege of screening Peter Miller's documentary that chronicles the use of anti-Semitic language against Jewish players in the early decades of baseball. The "F word" was an all-purpose insult thrown at everyone from Hall of Famer Hank Greenberg to bench guys. But Jewish players challenged fans and opponents, sometimes with their fists, until it was no longer part of the conversation. The same story can be told about Jackie Robinson, Roberto Clemente, and every player of color who had to hear insults in the heat of athletic battle until a combination of public and individual resistance made it an ugly memory.

Fast-forward to today: We have visible struggles for LGBT rights. We have a president who has finally "evolved" to support marriage equality. Hell, Focus on the Family announced that it was throwing in the towel on fighting LGBT marriage, admitting that they'd lost the under-thirty generation.[39] It would certainly help if more players came out of the closet. But one thing is certain: the big leagues can and need to do much more than just levy fines on players who happen to be caught speaking slurs on camera. NBA commissioner David Stern, who is a political liberal and a longtime friend of Rick Welts, said of gay rights, "I don't want to become a social crusader on this issue."[40] No kidding.

We don't need to see David Stern wave the rainbow flag (honestly, if it didn't have a swoosh on it, I don't think he ever would). But the commissioner could make discussion of homophobia part of every rookie orientation. How about a clear indication that homophobic language won't be tolerated any longer? How about statements from the NBA that if any rookies in the room happen to be gay, the NBA will stand as a workplace where their sexuality won't only be "tolerated" but embraced? On some level, the NBA understands that homophobia isn't good business. But for LGBT fans, writers, and players, and their families and friends, this isn't business; it's personal.

One thing is certain for both women *and* men: the vise of homophobia in sports will not loosen unless and until there is a movement off the field and in the streets.

Fighting gender-based prejudice in sports is fighting for a world where sports is about games, fun, and the thrill of teamwork, not about preparing our youth for war. It's about young girls in South Africa having the freedom to run without having to fear who will question their gender; it's about young boys in the United States who can be out and proud without giving up the right to play. It's about living in a world where our dignity and humanity are givens, not something to fight for. My favorite sign at the LGBT Equality March in DC read, "We hold these truths to be pretty frickin obvious!" This is absolutely right.

In the world of sports, there is still a ways to travel. If nothing else, however, we can see that if sports is the central arena where gender and sexual norms are enforced, then it can also be the place where they can most effectively be challenged. As NHL players say in their new ad campaign aimed at fighting homophobia, "If you can skate, you can play."

"I'm Not Your Child":
Racism Today in Sports

A 2011 poll found that Americans believe that professional sports are one of the *least* racist sectors in our society today.[1] This analysis cut across racial lines: all agreed that the world of sports is less racist than society as a whole. This raises two questions. First, why do people feel this way? And second, is it true?

The reason why people feel this way goes to the heart of what we are told and sold about sports—that, as famed sports journalist Red Smith put it, it is a "true meritocracy," where the color of your skin is irrelevant if you can produce on the field. We are told that racism, if it exists at all, is just a hangover from the days of trailblazers like Jackie Robinson and Muhammad Ali, who fought the good fight and led us into a more enlightened age.

This is, of course, wrong. It also obscures discussions worth having. Racism in sports is alive and well. If you want to see it emerge from the shadows, just speak out against it. Consider what happened when HBO *Real Sports* host Bryant Gumbel called NBA commissioner David Stern a "plantation overseer." Or take a look at the post-prison reform narrative of NFL star Michael Vick. Then there is what happens when sports tries to appropriate the civil rights struggles of the past to better market its present. We saw the crowd's reaction to musician Carlos Santana at Major League Baseball's annual Civil Rights Game when he talked about, well, civil rights. In 2012 we also enjoyed the emergence of Jeremy Lin, whose style of play and Taiwanese American heritage expanded the discussion about race and racism in U.S. sports and beyond. Finally, in the NHL playoffs, a fan's reaction to one of the few black professional players in the sport reminded us that so much of the past isn't past at all.

In all of this, we see the ways in which sports both is shaped by and shapes our society. If we accept that racism is still alive and well outside the arena, then sports would have to exist in a hermetically sealed, airtight environment in order to remain uninfected. Impossible. If we accept that, yes, race and racism are still live issues in sports, then we need to realize that how these issues are debated and discussed therein has a profound effect on how they are discussed and understood in our broader culture. Here's where it gets interesting. If reflections of racism are acknowledged as a reality in the world of sports, then how racism is challenged by athletes, sports journalists, and fans can have a positive ripple effect in challenging racism everywhere it occurs. It just so happens that some of the most interesting discussions about race over the last year have taken place through the prism of sports.

Plantation Politics

In October 2011, at the end of another episode of HBO's long-running series *Real Sports*, Bryant Gumbel referred to NBA commissioner David Stern as a "plantation overseer." The remarks added to an already simmering debate. At that time, the NBA players had been locked out for four months, negotiations were at a standstill, and a substantial part of the season was already canceled.

Many listeners were outraged. After all, how could the horrors of the slave trade possibly be compared to a billion-dollar labor negotiation? It's a fair question, but the metaphor—and the conflict it evokes—is as old as professional sports itself. In the nineteenth century, a white player named John Montgomery Ward was described as leading a "slave revolt" against Major League Baseball when he started the Players' League. In 1964, Muhammad Ali declared that he would "no longer be a slave." Five years later, the baseball player Curt Flood called himself "a well paid slave" because of his inability to exercise free agency (for which he went to court and lost both the case and his career). John Carlos always speaks of the day he raised his fist as the day when he "broke free from [his] shackles" and "found emancipation." Contemporary athletes such as Larry Johnson, Anthony Prior, Warren Sapp, and Adrian Peterson have used the formulation, as well. It's been deployed by players to describe a feeling of being condescended to—of being treated as boys instead of men—and of lacking control of their own livelihoods.

In the NBA, where every owner but one (Michael Jordan) is white and 86 percent of the players are black, racial tensions have remained unspoken but tangible. One scene during the labor negotiations vividly illustrates these tensions. According to ESPN's Ric Bucher, as David Stern sat across the table from a constellation of the league's stars, he became, per his usual style, openly contemptuous of the players' "inability to understand" the financial challenges faced by ownership. Stern rolled his eyes. He took deep breaths. He then pointed his finger repeatedly toward the face of the Miami Heat's Dwyane Wade.

Wade, who was then twenty-nine, is one of the most popular faces in the NBA. He interrupted Stern. "You're not pointing your finger at me," Wade said, according to Bucher. "I'm not your child."[2]

It's worth noting that Stern's résumé has all the trappings of a racial progressive. He's served on the board of the NAACP. He's led a league that has long had the best record of hiring people of color as coaches and executives. Even in terms of ownership, the NBA is the only major sport in which a person of African descent sits in a team's owner's box (although, since we're talking about the Charlotte Bobcats, we should probably put the word "team" in quotes). But none of that has protected Stern from the latest accusations, because these dynamics didn't develop overnight. For that, he bears most of the blame.

Over the last decade, Stern has built reservoirs of bad will. After an infamous 2004 brawl between members of the Indiana Pacers and fans of the Detroit Pistons, Stern said that he had a responsibility to "the ticket-buying fan" to clean up the league. He instituted a dress code that seemed like a direct concession to racial stereotypes, making it a finable offense for players to be photographed or interviewed wearing chains, medallions, or baggy jeans. He created a list of verboten establishments where players couldn't socialize when on the road. He set age limits on when players could enter the league. He met with the Republican strategist Matthew Dowd to discuss how to give the league "red state appeal." When he had the NBA's official magazine, *Hoop*, airbrush out Allen Iverson's tattoos, it was seen as an attack on the "hip-hop generation" of players. Yet Stern did little to reach out to them or address that perception.

What should be most maddening for the NBA's fans is that no one on the players' side trusted either Stern or the financial figures he repeatedly pointed to in negotiations. The league was coming off the most profitable season in its history, but Stern insisted that money was being hemorrhaged across the board. Players didn't believe him, especially since his solution to "the crisis of team profitability" was to take back money from the players themselves. Stern refused to consider a solution that would involve his owners sharing television revenue, as NFL teams do.

All this rightfully led to outrage, but the outrage was confused and at times even reflected the very racial tensions in the negotiating room. As the sportswriter Bill Simmons, writing for ESPN's *Grantland,* asked during the lockout, "Where's the big-picture leadership here? . . . I don't trust the players' side to make the right choices, because they are saddled with limited intellectual capital. (Sorry, it's true.) The owners' side can't say the same; they should be ashamed." The phrase "intellectual capital" had uglier echoes than Simmons may have intended. In response to criticism from several corners, including NBA players themselves, Simmons posted a clarification, noting, "If we're relying on someone to create a new economic model to save the league, don't expect it to be the players; it's outside their means. That's what I wrote. I would have written the same thing about NHL players, NFL players or MLB players."[3]

In other words, Simmons doubted the big-picture savvy and economic acuity of all athletes, not simply black athletes. I spoke to several NBA players on the negotiating team who made clear that they weren't assuaged by the explanation.

Racism reverberates with particular strength in the NBA because no other sport tries so aggressively to market African American players to an overwhelmingly white, middle-class "ticket-buying" audience. This dynamic causes a set of resentments and tensions that Stern seems unable to navigate. Instead of building bridges, he napalms them. Every scuffle, every fight, every elbow on the court is subject to the kind of hand-wringing that would be unheard of in fight-happy hockey. Every scandal is a commentary on the culture, attitudes, or even, as ESPN radio host Colin Cowherd opined, the "absence of fathers" in the African American community. In other words, race is discussed, but never explicitly—and never as a way of analyzing the assumptions of the analysts themselves. Instead, the discussion often merely reinforces racist attitudes about players, their backgrounds, and their states of mind.

The NFL is a league that is 70 percent African American, but it has done a remarkably effective job of marketing teams instead of individuals. For that reason, racism operates differently in the NFL. But it's still illustrative when we look at the curious case of Michael Vick.

Vick as Horatio Alger

Jackie Robinson, the man who broke baseball's color line, once said, "All these guys who were saying that we've got it made through athletics, it's just not so. You as an individual can make it, but I think we've got to concern ourselves with the masses of the people—not by what happens as an individual."[4] What does Jackie Robinson, a man on a U.S. postage stamp, possibly have in common with Michael Vick, who spent nearly two years in federal prison for being part of a dogfighting ring? The two men may be quite different, but the narratives built around them bear striking similarities.

At some point in 2011, Michael Vick became a Horatio Alger story. The vilified Vick morphed into our latest feel-good comeback hero, a symbol of this country's remarkable capacity for empathy and forgiveness. Vick signed a head-spinning six-year, $100 million contract with the Philadelphia Eagles, and the media narrative centered on the way he's been embraced by franchise and fans after falling so low.

Four years ago, Vick was making eleven cents an hour as a prison janitor in Leavenworth while serving time for his crime—a fact that is often mentioned in an offhand, "What a country!" manner. No doubt, the Vick journey is perhaps unrivaled in the history of sports. But take a moment to consider that eleven-cents-an-hour wage as a symptom of some larger, harsher realities. Michael Vick's janitorial job was just a subatomic particle of a prison labor–industrial complex intimately interwoven with the highest levels of corporate America.[5] The United States has more people behind bars than any country on earth. As David Fathi, the director of the ACLU's National Prisoner Project, commented, "Prisoners can be made to work, they don't have to be paid, and they lack the protections that free workers have, like workers' compensation and the right to join a union. So there's a real potential for exploitation and abuse."[6]

Among African American men, like Vick, the numbers incarcerated stagger the senses. As Michelle Alexander, bestselling author of *The New Jim Crow,* points out, more African American men are incarcerated, on probation, or on parole than were enslaved in 1850, a decade before the Civil War.[7] David Fathi also pointed out to me that "most Americans know that the Thirteenth Amendment outlawed slavery and involuntary servitude. What many don't know is that it contains an exception for prisoners." In fact, a mind-boggling number of private companies, from Kmart and JCPenney to McDonald's and Wendy's, outsource to U.S. prisons.[8] When you call American Airlines or Avis, the person helping you with your travel might be chained to a desk. As Liliana Segura, a board member at the Campaign to End the Death Penalty, noted, "There's a reason people call it modern day slavery. . . . Prisoners represent nothing less than a massive—and expanding—invisible workforce in this country."

So, yes, Michael Vick has gone from eleven cents an hour to the $100 million man—but for the mass of prisoners who can't run forty yards in 4.4 seconds or throw a ball sixty yards with a flick of the wrist, the future is bleak. That's why we should remember Jackie Robinson's words: if we would "concern ourselves with the masses of the people," then we'd properly view Michael Vick's ascension as cause for reflection, not celebration. He made it out of the prison system intact. His story is exceptional because millions of people won't be able to say the same—because that's not what generally happens when you're caught in a system that measures your worth at eleven cents an hour.

The Politics of Standing Up

In the confederate confines of sports radio, casual bigotry is about as common as traffic updates. Far less common, even unprecedented, is for a manager or coach to call out a member of the media's comments as racist. That's exactly what San Francisco Giants manager Bruce Bochy did to nationally syndicated sports radio talker Tony Bruno, and he should be applauded for it. After Bochy's pitcher Ramon Ramirez hit Shane Victorino of the Philadelphia Phillies, sparking a bench-clearing brawl, Bruno blew a gasket. He posted "Giants Bochy is a coward for having his illegal alien pitcher hit a guy."

Ramirez, of course, is not an "illegal" anything. Like each of the 30 percent of Major League players who aren't citizens, he lives and works here under a P-1 visa, often referred to as an entertainment visa. But then, no human being is "illegal" at all. It's just an ugly slur that's been mainstreamed by those who target the undocumented. As Gustavo Andrade, the organizing director of leading immigrant rights group Casa de Maryland, said to me, "Mr. Bruno was clearly not making a factual statement about Mr. Ramirez's immigration status; rather, he was making a derogatory comment about him based on his race. . . . Mr. Bruno's tweet was racist, ignorant and dangerous. It propagates the idea that all Latinos are somehow less than human."

When Bochy heard about Bruno's comments, he was incensed, saying, "Forget the remarks about me. That doesn't bother me. For a guy to make a racist comment like that and have the ear of so many people, that bothers me. I can defend myself as a coward. I don't know if you can defend yourself making a racist comment."[9]

After the initial uproar, Bruno set a land-speed record for issuing a classic "non-apology apology," where he slammed "the sheep on facebook, twitter and blogs." Later, Bruno wrote, "I did remove my post and apologize for my comments regarding illegal aliens. I was angry and on the air and I stand behind my comments that Bruce Bochy is a coward, as are all managers who order pitchers to throw at guys just because their pitchers can't get a guy out. All of you people resorting to name calling are more classless and vile."[10] You could almost weep over the heartfelt remorse.

Presumably one of those "more classless and vile" people is Alex Nogales, president of the National Hispanic Media Coalition, who said of Bruno, "This guy is a pig. In this day and age, using this kind of language, which encourages intolerance and hate crimes, is inexcusable."[11] Honestly, I disagree with Nogales. I disagree because his comments are highly insulting to pigs, who are extremely intelligent animals. I bet Bruno couldn't find a quality truffle if his life depended on it.

The question at hand, though, is whether Bruno should be fired. I asked Dr. Carlos Munoz Jr., ethnic studies professor at UC Berkeley, who said, "Comments like his are harmful because they perpetuate the racist anti-immigrant hysteria that exists throughout the nation. It adds fuel to the fire that started burning in Arizona and that has expanded to Georgia and other states. He deserves to be fired." When you host a national radio show, racism, ignorance, and abject stupidity are, in fact, firing offenses.

But the unfortunate words of one don't change the fact that this whole sorry story comes back to the political climate around the game. Responsibility for that falls at the feet of baseball commissioner Bud Selig. Under Selig's watch, teams have invested billions in the Dominican Republic and Venezuela to develop talent on the cheap. Yet he does nothing to recognize the humanity of the players who are the game's brightest stars. Selig has had several opportunities to prove that he considers Latino players more than just a talent pool. But he rejected the movement to retire Roberto Clemente's number 21 in every park. He refused to remain in the stadium and talk to reporters when Carlos Santana spoke out against anti-Latino bigotry at the 2011 Civil Rights Game. Most egregiously and unforgivably, he wouldn't move the 2011 All-Star Game out of Arizona despite the state's evolution as a place where Latino players and fans are simply unsafe.

In Bud Selig's baseball universe, Roberto Clemente goes unrecognized and people like Tony Bruno enjoy national platforms to slander "illegal aliens." We may be able to get Tony Bruno off the air, but there is a bigger fight brewing for the very soul of the National Pastime. Will baseball be a force for inclusion or exclusion? Throughout its checkered history, this game has certainly been both. Right now, Bud stands with Tony Bruno on the wrong side of that history.

The Hope of Jeremy Lin

By the time you read this, Jeremy Lin could have become a bench fixture, been seriously felled by an injury, or merely faded away. That's the beauty and cruelty of sports: there are simply no sure things. But even in the worst-case scenario, Jeremy Lin has already made history, both on the court and off. On the court, the former New York Knicks and current Houston Rockets point guard set a record for most points in NBA history in just his first five starts. Think about that. This record isn't held by MJ, Kareem, or LeBron; it's held by Jeremy Lin.

Lin is also the first American-born player of Chinese-Taiwanese descent ever in the NBA, as well as a Harvard graduate. But he plays with a blacktop flair that defies preconception and prejudice. The fact that he did this all in New York City only added to the hype. And, along with a thousand puns on his name—Linsanity!— Jeremy Lin's game spawned some of the most interesting, as well as awkward, discussions on race and racism the sports world has ever managed.

It's no surprise that Lin has become a magnet for attention. On one hand, he's part of a tradition of NBA players who don't fit into stereotypical boxes. Remember Jason "White Chocolate" Williams, the tattooed Caucasian with game courtesy of Rucker Park? Seven-foot long-range shooters like Dirk Nowitzki, or diminutive players like Muggsy Bogues, Spud Webb, and Earl Boykins, or tall point guards from Magic Johnson to Penny Hardaway all drew attention initially because they possessed the shock of the new. No sport is as naked as the NBA, with faces and bodies on full display for crowded fans and HD cameras; when someone breaks a superficial mold, attention will follow. And sometimes, breaking this mold leads to a bizarre racial panic. Jason Whitlock, from Fox Sports, tweeted a racist "joke" about Jeremy Lin, for which he had to quickly apologize. People sent out all manner of "I thought Asians couldn't drive!" tweets and messages. A "yellow mamba" sign was spotted at Madison Square Garden. Boxer Floyd Mayweather said, "Jeremy Lin is a good player but all the hype is because he's Asian. Black players do what he does every night and don't get the same praise."[12]

This is simply not true. Lin's statistics, at the time of Mayweather's statement, were beyond what any player—black, brown, or white—had ever done in his NBA launch. This kind of panic is something we've seen historically in sports when a marginalized person not only breaks into the party but outdoes everyone attending.

One hundred years ago, when Jack Johnson became the first African American heavyweight champion, he defied notions of white supremacy, such as the belief that African Americans lack the intelligence to apply strategy and smarts to sports. We can say the same about Jackie Robinson, who did more than just break baseball's color barrier and win Rookie of the Year in 1947. Robinson played with a grace under pressure that challenged white—and even many black—preconceptions about mental toughness on the highest stage. In addition, he did so while playing with an energy that forever changed the game. Or consider Martina Navratilova. Yes, she blazed trails just by being an out and proud LGBT champion tennis player. But she also played with a muscled strength and swagger that changed women's sports forever. The Williams sisters owe as much to Martina as they do to Arthur Ashe and Althea Gibson.

There have been other pioneering Asian American players, notably Wataru "Wat" Misaka. There have been biracial players of Asian descent: Raymond Townsend, Corey Gaines, Rex Walters, and Robert Swift. There have been Chinese-national players who have made a big impact, such as Yao Ming.

But it's not Lin's name that makes him stand out. It's his game. It's not just that he's a cultural curio, an Asian American from Harvard in the NBA. It's the way he breaks ankles and swaggers down the court after draining a game-winning three-pointer. Asian Americans are stereotypically framed as studious and reserved. We would expect nothing more than for an Asian American player to be robotic and fundamentally sound, his face an unsmiling mask. Instead, we have Jeremy Lin threading no-look passes, dunking, and, in the most respected mark of toughness, taking contact and finishing baskets. As ESPN's Michael Yam said, "The special people are the ones who pave the path and that's what Lin is doing for every Asian American who is watching his every move on the court. . . . He is humble, well spoken and a leader who has made every Asian who doesn't 'look' the part believe in his or her abilities. In my career I have had people look at me and doubt my skills as a broadcaster."[13]

But most impressive—and transgressive—is that Lin plays with a flair that in only a few games gave a dour, mopey Knicks team a renewed sense of purpose and joy. His pre-game handshakes alone have more intelligent soul than Donald Glover.

As sports columnists struggled to figure out how to discuss Lin, they reached for the easiest possible comparison: Tim Tebow. Every sports columnist with opposable thumbs (about three in ten) has compared Lin and the then–Denver Broncos quarterback. The *Wall Street Journal* sports page published an entire column about their similarities. Sportswriter Bill Simmons used the rapier wit that made him famous and summed up the general consensus by tweeting, "My Tebowner has been replaced by a Jerection!" And it wasn't just sports columnists. Politico, our national source for electoral CliffsNotes, and the Huffington Post, America's go-to site for finding out what Fabio thinks about education reform, both proclaimed, "Lin is the new Tebow."

The comparison is understandable. Both players revived depressed franchises just by getting in the game. Both play with a joy that seems to infect their teammates and raise everyone's level of play. Both had their doubters, no question. And both are devout Christians who aren't shy about thanking God in post-game interviews.

It's an easy comparison. It's also dead wrong. The conflation of their stories does little more than burnish Tebow's credentials at Lin's expense. Let's really look at both players. Tim Tebow was a first-round draft pick who won a Heisman Trophy and two national championships at football powerhouse Florida. Jeremy Lin was an undrafted player out of Harvard, cut by two other teams and riding the Knicks' bench before his unprecedented emergence. Tim Tebow had an army of supporters chanting his name and exhorting the front office to get him on the field. Jeremy Lin played because the Knicks had no other options. Tim Tebow, based on pure statistics, just isn't very good yet: he completed 46 percent of his passes and ranked twenty-seventh among NFL quarterbacks in passing efficiency in 2011. Jeremy Lin is at a different level.

But it's for reasons completely disconnected from statistics that the differences blare like a siren. Sure, Jeremy Lin is a person of faith—but Tim Tebow does commercials for Focus on the Family and believes his faith gives him the right to bury the rights of others.

Then there's the fact—not to shock anyone—that Jeremy Lin is Asian American. Clearly, this and the Ivy League pedigree made scouts disinclined to see what is crystal clear: the man has game for days. I and many others saw it in the 2010 Summer League, when Lin traded blows with number one overall pick John Wall. Lin's skills didn't appear overnight, just his opportunity. Tim Tebow always had the benefit of the doubt. Jeremy Lin was just doubted.

There are soft liberal sportswriters who say primly that they don't notice color and just like Lin's game. Gene Lyons, writing for Salon, said, "Look, Jeremy Lin is a fellow fortunate enough to make a handsome living putting an inflated rubber ball through an iron hoop, as millions of his clumsier brethren dreamed of doing in our youth. . . . It has no transcendental meaning. It's a ballgame."[14]

Hogwash. If they don't acknowledge it, then the discussion is ceded to those with a racist ax to grind. We then get to only talk about it in the context of one of Jason Whitlock's racist jokes—or when the biggest sports channel around made one of its more egregious missteps in years.

Outrage erupted when ESPN's website posted a headline that read, "Chink in the Armor." Seriously. An ESPN anchor had previously used the same phrase in an interview with Knicks Hall of Fame guard Walt Frazier, and it had also been uttered on ESPN radio. But the Web page was captured and the frozen image went viral. ESPN quickly posted a statement as bloodless as it was insufficient:

Last night, ESPN.com's mobile web site posted an offensive headline referencing Jeremy Lin at 2:30 am ET. The headline was removed at 3:05 am ET. We are conducting a complete review of our cross-platform editorial procedures and are determining appropriate disciplinary action to ensure this does not happen again. We regret and apologize for this mistake.[15]

After outrage ensued, another statement assured readers that the headline writer had been fired and the anchor had been suspended for thirty days.[16] There are only two conclusions to draw from all of this. Either ESPN has a group of outright racists sitting at the *SportsCenter* desk, hosting their radio shows, and writing headlines—doubtful—or the people in question have no antiracist mental apparatus for how to talk about an Asian American player. As a result, we see again that people of Asian descent are subject to a casual racism that other ethnic groups don't have to suffer quite as starkly.

No one at ESPN would talk or write about a lesbian athlete and unconsciously put forth that the woman in question would have a "finger in the dike." If an African American player was thought of as stingy, it's doubtful that anyone at the "Worldwide Leader in Sports" would describe that person as "niggardly." They would never brand a member of a football team as a "Redskin." (Wait, scratch that last one.)

They wouldn't do it because a mental synapse would spark to life and signal that today, unless you're speaking at CPAC, that's just not OK. This collective synapse was forged by mass movements for black and LGBT liberation in this country that have forced a lot of people, particularly white straight men, to have a clue. But there simply hasn't been a similar national struggle built by people of Asian descent. I spoke about this with William Wong, a longtime journalist born and raised in Oakland's Chinatown, who said,

We haven't had a national mass Asian American civil rights movement because our numbers have been small and diffuse thanks to various exclusionary and discriminatory laws. Our communities are also too diverse in terms of American history and intra-Asian cultural and political differences. But we should note that many Asian Americans in the 1960s, 1970s, and 1980s were energized by the larger civil rights movement to organize an Asian American movement in states like California, Washington, and New York where we had the numbers to come together.

This is true. In places with concentrations of people willing to stand up, Asian Americans have come together across differences of language and origin to demand respect and equal rights, often in the face of violence.

Lin's having "no transcendental meaning" would be news to many, including Wong; Jeff Chang, author of the award-winning *Can't Stop Won't Stop: A History of the Hip-Hop Generation* and the forthcoming *Who We Be: The Colorization of America;* and Helen Gym, a board member at Asian Americans United in Philadelphia. Wong made it plain: "There's never been a Jeremy Lin in our collective community history. After the California Gold Rush, a century's worth of legal discrimination and racist violence, we finally have our first sports superstar."

Lin's emergence has initiated the national dialogue that people of Asian descent have craved for some time. Helen Gym told me about the moment when she felt the discussion became bigger than basketball, recounting, "When the Knicks defeated the Lakers and Jason Whitlock put up his racist tweet, there was such an outpouring of support and such an overwhelming rejection of a long-held racial stereotype. I couldn't keep up with my Twitter feed anymore, and I couldn't put it down. I think I fell asleep with my phone in my hand."

As Gym describes, this tidal wave of celebration, as well as anti-racist vigilance, speaks to sentiments that have been simmering for years but until now only found expression at the local level. "Jeremy Lin has galvanized a vocal and sharply politicized Asian America which is going directly to bat on anti-Asian slurs, stereotyping, and racist frameworks that have marginalized our community," continued Gym. "The fact that Lin doesn't shy away from talking about anti-Asian stereotypes that have impacted his career has driven home the impact of such stereotypes in a deeply personal way. . . . I am just as proud of a new generation of Asian Americans that has not only rallied around Lin but is articulating a distinct Asian American experience and identity and shifting the discussion toward a more multiracial understanding of this country."

Lin has provided space for discussions not only about contemporary racism but about Asian American history, as well—from forgotten pro basketball trailblazers like Wat Misaka to the critical (and often overlooked) role people of Asian descent played in building the American left. They were some of the original members of the Industrial Workers of the World, and they were founding members of the United Farm Workers as well as the Black Panther Party. Lin's ascendance, even if there is no evidence that he is politically active, has allowed these discussions to come to light.

Even Lin's style of play has provoked discussions that push beyond his on-court brilliance. Lin moves with a confidence and cool more akin to the African American basketball aesthetic, an example of the kind of cross-cultural hybridization that is common in the United States but so often unacknowledged. William Wong thinks this alone holds remarkable potential, saying,

> He has a chance to be a model for positive social relationships between blacks and Asians. These relationships range from

loving, copacetic, friendly and respectful to alienated, hostile, suspicious and hateful. Now that Lin is playing smoothly with a lot of black basketballers and doing it in a way that is inclusive and collaborative—and winning the respect of many black players—he could be a prime symbol of racial reconciliation for the young generation, and offer a lesson for elders of all racial and ethnic backgrounds.

But the most important part of Lin's emergence is that, in the middle of all the sideline giggling and chest bumping, he is first and foremost the stellar point guard Jeremy Lin. This is at the heart of Linsanity. It's not just the Asian American piece; it's not the Harvard piece. It's not even the flair. It's that when Lin is doing his thing, you see his grin and feel the joy. Lin has signed with the Houston Rockets. But for now we can relish the memory of Linsanity and a player who breaks the ultimate stereotype: he makes tired NBA players look like they're having the time of their lives.

The question is, what happens now? Every sports/culture/political writer has tried to grab a little bit of Jeremy Lin's shine; we have yet to see whether those who rushed to stand with Lin will stand up for him as well. One thing is certain: Lin has done more than bring hope to aspiring athletes of Asian descent. He holds the promise of making visible masses of people who have been deemed irrelevant by decades of racism. At a time when hope is in short supply, Lin speaks to the best angels of our nature, and in so doing, he inspires progress and change. As Chang says, "Part of me is over all the chatter about what Jeremy means, but the other part of me realizes that we've just turned a page in the way Asian-Americans are represented in the United States."

Joel Ward Meets the Boston Bruins Faithful

A moment of sports euphoria turned decidedly ugly after the underdog Washington Capitals beat the reigning Boston Bruins 2–1 in game seven of the 2012 Stanley Cup quarterfinals series. Before disbelieving eyes, the Caps' Joel Ward scored the winning overtime goal against 2011's Stanley Cup hero, Tim Thomas. But Ward is black, and before you could even utter "postracial," self-identifying Bruin fans had tweeted a cascade of ugly invective, with the "N-word" their epithet of choice.[17]

Tim Thomas is the player who created a sports media firestorm when he refused to join his team and meet with President Obama after the Bruins won the 2011 Stanley Cup. To be clear, I have zero problems with athletes refusing to be part of presidential photo ops. But Thomas's political reasons are not irrelevant to what caused the recent spasm of hate against Ward. Thomas is a proud financial supporter of the Tea Party. He counts Glenn Beck as a hero and once emblazoned the "Don't Tread on Me" flag on his helmet. When asked by reporters why he wouldn't meet with Obama, Thomas didn't comment and instead referred people to his Facebook page, which had a paragraph on the "out of control Federal government."[18]

To see no connection between the Tea Party, Glenn Beck, and the politics of racial resentment is to subscribe to either blind ignorance or political cowardice. (Even Beck, last December, inferred that racism in the Tea Party drives anti-Obama animus.[19])

After the Caps-Bruins showdown, senior ESPN writer Howard Bryant told me,

> The goal itself wasn't particularly important. [Barbadian-Canadian] Anson Carter was a Boston playoff hero during the 1999 playoffs. The significance of Ward's goal is that the man

he beat, Tim Thomas, has through his thinly veiled racism undermined what should be a glorious revival of hockey in Boston. . . . Thomas by himself turned new Boston into old Boston, and the embarrassing fan response to Ward's goal proved it.

As much as many from New England would like to forget it, "old Boston" is a core part of this story. No city in the United States has a more tortured intersection of race and sports than the supposed cradle of liberalism and democracy. It's the city whose Red Sox were the last team to integrate, waiting until 1959, twelve years after Jackie Robinson broke through with the Brooklyn Dodgers. It's the city that for decades rejected the greatest team basketball player in history, Bill Russell, because of his proud, unblinking opposition to racial intolerance. After dealing with years of everything from verbal abuse to the vandalizing of his home, Russell called the city "a flea market of racism."[20] Boston then embraced Larry Bird to such a passionate degree that his very jersey became a symbol of white arrogance, exemplified in Spike Lee's *Do the Right Thing*. Boston is also paradoxically (and fittingly for a city this paradoxical) the first hockey town to integrate, when Willie O'Ree took the ice for the Bruins in 1958 (he would be the NHL's last black player for sixteen years). Now when Joel Ward plays the hero, the reflex is the "N" bomb. As Faulkner said, "The past is not dead. It isn't even past."

Of course, racism is not a "Boston thing." Of course, the sewers of the Internet overflow with bile if you have the stomach to look. Besides, we've collectively witnessed the character assassination of the slain Trayvon Martin, with no regard for either his humanity or his grieving parents, so we should probably refrain from being too shocked. As sports writer Bomani Jones tweeted when people pointed out the anti-Ward hate, "Folks called a n-word repeatedly behind a dead teenager. of course someone would say it over a game 7."

None of that, however, should blind us from the basic truth: racism is a reality in sports, as in life. We can choose to ignore it, but that only guarantees that it will continue, both in sports and outside of it.

After the game, Thomas and the Bruins stayed on the ice, waited for the Caps celebrations to die down, and congratulated their opponents. When speaking to the media, neither Thomas nor his teammates exhibited anything but class. There were no excuses, no resentments.

Perhaps this is why Americans of every color believe sports to be less racist than the rest of society: the humble acts of sportsmanship in full view of the millions watching. These simple, old-fashioned gestures say, "After the final buzzer, we are equals." The truth, as we have seen, is much more complicated—as complicated inside the lines as it is outside of them.

Post-Game

The last several years will be remembered for their rebellions. Words like "occupy" have reached as far as the sports pages, and new voices in the sports world are straining to be heard. The stakes, as I wrote in the introduction, have never been higher.

They are higher than merely the political footprint an athlete leaves behind or whether or not their hyperexalted platform is put to good use. The stakes are high because the sports community and its journalists are today regularly dealing with issues of life and death, and seem completely unprepared for the task. At the time of this writing, on May 2, 2012, one of the great men in NFL history, Junior Seau, committed suicide. While we don't know why Seau took his own life, the stubborn facts around his death can't be ignored.

We know that Seau was the NFL's second suicide in two weeks, after former Atlanta Falcon Ray Easterling killed himself on April 19. We know that Seau took his life by shooting himself in the chest, and not the head—which happened to be former Chicago Bears safety Dave Duerson's method of choice in February 2011. According to Duerson's much-publicized final note, he said he was putting a bullet in his heart instead of his head so his brain could be sent to the Boston University School of Medicine for study. His family complied, and it was found that Duerson suffered from a neurodegenerative disease associated with concussions. Medical professionals link these injuries to depression, early-onset Alzheimer's, and, as a tragic corollary, suicide. Duerson's family is now suing the league in a wrongful-death suit.

We also now know that not once in twenty years was Seau ever diagnosed with a concussion on an injury report. This is either a miracle akin to dancing between raindrops, or Seau and team doctors simply didn't report concussions when they occurred. When asked if her husband had ever suffered a concussion, Seau's ex-wife Gina told ESPN, "Of course he had. He always bounced back and kept on playing. He's a warrior. That didn't stop him. I don't know what football player hasn't. It's not ballet. It's part of the game."[1]

We know that while Seau was not part of the more than fifteen hundred players suing the NFL for misleading them about head injuries and their possible effects, he was sympathetic to their cause. In a heartbreaking column, *Sports Illustrated*'s Jim Trotter reflected on the passing of his dear friend. He also revealed Seau's thoughts about head injuries, as well as his response to those who say that new safety rules are making the sport "too soft." "Those who are saying the game is changing for the worse, well, they don't have a father who can't remember his name because of the game," Seau said to Trotter. "I'm pretty sure if everybody had to wake with their dad not knowing his name, not knowing his kids' name, not being able to function at a normal rate after football, they would understand that the game needs to change."[2]

Seau could have been describing Ray Easterling's world. The former Atlanta Falcons safety was a lead plaintiff in one of the class-action lawsuits against the NFL. In a heartbreaking *New York Times* article, Ray Easterling's wife, Mary Ann, described the last twenty years of their marriage:

No adverse aftereffects surfaced through the 1980s. Ray's engaging personality, discipline and diligence proved a good formula in the financial services field. What followed was a downward spiral during which he flipped to being argumentative and forgetful, as if a personality transplant were mixed in with the two dozen orthopedic operations he endured. Business ventures slid off the rails when Ray, for whom punctuality was a practiced virtue, appeared tardy for appointments. In many settings, he would blurt out offensive remarks, the filter in his brain no longer functioning at full tilt. Realizing this, he became disengaged, even from his mother, who died a month before he did. At family events, he would show up in running shorts when more formal attire was appropriate. Staring into space wistfully, Mary Ann said, "I didn't feel like I was with the person that I married."[3]

As the Duerson, Seau, and Easterling families mourn, however, players who speak out about head injuries are still subject to immense ridicule. The NFL is the biggest game in town, and it's been a political story in itself to watch the media and many former players fall over themselves to "defend the shield." When former MVP Kurt Warner, who was forced out of football because of concussions, said that he wouldn't want his own son playing tackle football, former player Merril Hoge called him "irresponsible and unacceptable."[4]

Warner responded as anything but, writing,

In a world where perception is reality, you can imagine the kinds of pressures in professional sports. The pressure can be personal, when a player doesn't want to let down his teammates by sitting out a game. The pressure can be peer-driven, borne of the looks from coaches and players that say, "you

need to be on the field for us." Then there is the pressure
for many marginal players to get out there and play or their
entire career could be over. Yet probably the most demanding pressure is that those playing football are supposed to be
tough—and we all know that tough means having the ability
to play through injury. Those who place their pain aside and
line up next to their teammates for battle gain instant rec-
ognition from their team and fans. Nobody in this business
wants to be recognized as "soft."[5]

Then Brandon Marshall, the former all-pro wide receiver with
the Chicago Bears, stepped in and raised the issue of mental
health, writing in the *Chicago Sun-Times,*

> As I began to meditate more on Junior's death, I began to
> think about this vicious cycle our world is in. . . . The cycle
> starts when we are young boys and girls. Let me illustrate it
> for you: Li'l Johnny is outside playing and falls. His dad tells
> him to get up and be strong, to stop crying because men don't
> cry. So even from the age of 2 . . . we are teaching our boys
> not to show weakness or share any feelings or emotions, other
> than to be strong and tough. Is that "validating"?[6]

The crisis in the NFL and the players' response also opened up
an important discussion about research that shows women to be
silent victims of concussions and other slow-burn injuries. As one
study showed, "female athletes suffer more symptoms and recover
more slowly than males. . . . Research shows that doctors and train-
ers don't conduct follow-up exams with female athletes as quickly
as they do with males, either."[7]

This all points to the bigger issue, which is that the pain associated with playing high-level sports is largely hidden from the

audience. Since we don't need to confront the costs of violence, we then send our own children into the sports world with a highly distorted idea of what actually goes on when the cameras are off.

Athletes are stepping up to discuss this, and we are all better off for it. We are better off for reasons even beyond being able to make informed decisions about whether we or our children play sports. We are better off because we live in a world where these very attitudes—from the stigmas attached to mental illness to stereotypical conceptions of gender—are burdens we all share, in one way or another. Athletes can open up space to have conversations that otherwise wouldn't happen. This is also the case, as I hope I've shown, with issues of racism, workers' rights, and even grander narratives of solidarity and revolution. This thing so many have dismissed as "just sports" is—more than music, more than art—the closest thing to common language we have as human beings.

There is another reason why hearing athletes speak out on these issues matters. This is about their lives, as well. The idea, whether held by jocks or fans, that they live in a citadel away from these concerns is profoundly foolish. In the Palestinian territories, two national team players, Ayman Alkurd and Wajeh Moshate, were killed during the bombing of Gaza. The national stadium was destroyed. Another player on that national team, Gaza native Mahmoud Sarsak, was jailed for three years and no one knows why, other than that he is a prominent Gaza citizen whom Israel has deemed a threat. As of this writing, he was recently released, but only after a hunger strike that almost took his life, an international outcry from Amnesty international, and a formal written protest by FIFpro—a union of 50,000 professional soccer players. For a Palestinian athlete, the question about whether or not to be political is not an option.

In the United States, athletes are fortunately not faced with such hellish choices. But Jeremy Lin has to navigate racism. Danica

Patrick has to navigate sexism. The prospect of any athlete's coming out of the closet is a political minefield. The choices these athletes face—and how they face them—have a ripple effect we'd be terribly wrong to deny. To ignore everything that has happened over the last two years means to also ignore the way masses of people might be digesting these issues. At the end of the day, sports is a cultural arena that we ignore only at our collective peril.

Sure, we may desire for sports to be solely about play. But here's the thing: this cheapens not only the deep relevance of sports to our society but also the courage of those athletes who do take a stand. We do an injustice to all of them—and to what's best about sports—when we sanitize the past and rip athletics out of the political and cultural context in which it has always belonged. This is why the courageous stands of Muhammad Ali retain their wicked daring to this day. This is why I remain so inspired by John Carlos and Tommie Smith and the Fists of Freedom at the 1968 Olympics. They paid an awful price for their actions, but today they are heroes for what they did. When John Carlos is asked if he has regrets, he says, "I don't have regrets. The people with regrets are the ones at 1968 who agreed with us and did nothing."

Keeping our mouths shut in the face of injustice may help us ridicule others, or silence them, or assure ourselves that we stay popular with those cloistered keepers of "normality." But real courage means standing up when it's not popular—and real men and real women don't ask permission to raise their fists.

* * * * *

This is a book about athletes who have recently dared to speak out on topics having nothing to do with sports and everything to do with social justice. Only three months after I finished putting this book together, another tale emerged that I had no choice but to include. This story alone shows that we are making unprecedented progress.

Baltimore Raven Brendon Ayanbadejo, mentioned in an ear-lier chapter, is an NFL player proudly outspoken in his support of marriage equality and LGBT rights. As a Maryland resident, Ayanbadejo has contributed time, money, and even an online video to a November ballot initiative for Maryland to be the next state to recognize same-sex marriage. This was too much for Baltimore County state delegate Emmett Burns. Burns, a Democrat, sent a formal letter to Ravens team owner Steve Biscotti stating, "I find it inconceivable that one of your players, Mr. Brendon Ayanbadejo, would publicly endorse Same-Sex marriage, specifically, as a Raven Football player. . . . I believe Mr. Ayanbadejo should concentrate on football and steer clear of dividing the fan base." Then Burns went even farther and requested that Biscotti "take the necessary action, as a National Football Franchise Owner, to inhibit such expressions from your employees and that [Ayanbadejo] be ordered to cease and desist such injurious actions. I know of no other NFL player who has done what Mr. Ayanbadejo is doing."[8]

Yes, you read that correctly: Burns, an elected official, is calling on Ayanbadejo's boss to coerce him to shut up.

It's worth noting that Burns's last statement just isn't true. Play-ers such as Scott Fujita, NFL Hall of Famer Michael Irvin, the entire San Francisco 49ers team, and even *Sports Illustrated* NFL preview cover boy Rob Gronkowski have all spoken out for LGBT rights. Ayanbadejo responded to Burns forcefully, defending his own freedom of expression and telling *USA Today*, "It's an equality issue. I see the big picture. There was a time when women didn't have rights. Black people didn't have rights. Right now, gay rights is a big issue and it's been for a long time. We're slowly chopping down the barriers to equality."[9]

But the greatest response to Burns—and perhaps to anything in the history of everything—was made by Minnesota Vikings punter Chris Kluwe. Kluwe happens to believe in LGBT rights, as well as the rights of athletes to speak their minds. The punter sat down at his computer and produced the greatest political statement since Muhammad Ali told the U.S. government that "the real enemy of my people is here." Perhaps that's hyperbole. Certainly it's arguable. But what's undeniable is the greatness of Kluwe's rant.

(Warning: it's brilliantly profane, or profanely brilliant, so you might not want to print it out at work and leave it lying around. Then again, if you work in a place with NFL fans prone to homophobic slurs, you might want to leave it everywhere.)

Kluwe begins by calling out Burns for his "vitriolic hatred and bigotry." He then schools Burns on the Constitution, the First Amendment, and the history of racism and segregation in the NFL. People should find it and read it in its entirety. But the coup de grâce is his defense of LGBT equality. Kluwe writes:

> I can assure you that gay people getting married will have zero effect on your life. They won't come into your house and steal your children. They won't magically turn you into a lustful c—kmonster. They won't even overthrow the government in an orgy of hedonistic debauchery because all of a sudden they have the same legal rights as the other 90 percent of our population—rights like Social Security benefits, child care tax credits, Family and Medical Leave to take care of loved ones, and COBRA healthcare for spouses and children. You know what having these rights will make gays? Full-fledged American citizens just like everyone else, with the freedom to pursue happiness and all that entails. Do the civil-rights struggles of the past 200 years mean absolutely nothing to you?
>
> In closing, I would like to say that I hope this letter, in some small way, causes you to reflect upon the magnitude of the colossal foot in mouth clusterf—ck you so brazenly unleashed on a man whose only crime was speaking out for

something he believed in. Best of luck in the next election; I'm fairly certain you might need it.

Sincerely,

Chris Kluwe[10]

For the first time in football history, a punter is truly leading the way. Thank you, Chis Kluwe, for the gutsiest political statement made by any athlete in decades. The fact that it happens to be about LGBT rights only shows how far we've traveled, in the streets and in the locker rooms. Cyd Zeigler, a founder of Outsports.com, said, "It was unexpected to a lot of gay people to have someone from the most masculine sports league in the country come to the defense of the gay community and attack this person. It was unexpected, and it was awesome."

That sums up much of the last two years in the collision of sports and politics: unexpected, but also awesome. Politics has indeed turned the sports world upside down—but the funny thing about being upside down is that you can discover a whole new perspective.

Notes

PRE-GAME

1. Jorge Rivas, "Judge Revokes Bail for George Zimmerman in Trayvon Martin Case," *Colorlines*, June 1, 2012.
2. https://twitter.com/KingJames/statuses/183243305428058112.
3. Associated Press, "Wade, Heat speak out on shooting death of Florida teen," March 24, 2012, http://www.nba.com/2012/news/03/23/heat-statement.ap/index.html.
4. Ibid.
5. Dave Zirin, "LeBron James and the Perils of Walking the Fence," *The Nation*, October 4, 2010, http://www.thenation.com/blog/155162/lebron-james-and-perils-walking-fence.
6. Vincent Goodwill, "Pistons Players Reflect on Teen's Death," *Detroit News*, March 28, 2012.
7. Mike Hale, "An Olympic Champion, a Symbol and an Awkward Partner with Fame," *New York Times*, April 30, 2012, http://tv.nytimes.com/2012/05/01/arts/television/jesse-owens-on-pbss-american-experience.html.
8. Howard Cosell and Peter Bonventre, *I Never Played the Game* (New York: HarperCollins, 1985).
9. Jon Wertheim, "More Athletes Taking Political Stands," Sports Illustrated.com, September 9, 2008, http://sportsillustrated.cnn.com/2008/writers/jon_wertheim/09/09/activism/.
10. "Chris Douglas-Roberts offers different perspective on death of Osama bin Laden," SportingNews.com, May 2, 2011, http://aol.sportingnews.com/nba/story/2011-05-02/chris-douglas-roberts-offers-different-perspective-on-death-of-osama-bin-laden#ixzz1x73rdDOc.

11. Don Banks, "Mendenhall just the latest NFL player to spout utter nonsense," SportsIllustrated.com, May 4, 2011, http://sportsillus trated.cnn.com/2011/writers/don_banks/05/04/mendenhall/index.html #ixzz1x74NNgJQ.
12. Vinnie Iyer, "Rooney responds to Mendenhall's tweets about bin Laden," SportingNews.com, May 3, 2011, http://aol.sportingnews .com/nfl/story/2011-05-03/rooney-responds-to-mendenhalls-tweets -about-bin-laden#ixzz1x74xUirn.

1: OCCUPY THE SPORTS WORLD

1. Jon Saraceno, "For Packers' Mike McCarthy, there's no pressure for re-peat," *USA Today*, February 2, 2011, http://www.usatoday.com/sports/ football/nfl/packers/2011-02-07-mike-mccarthy-monday_N.htm.
2. Jason Stein, "Gov. Walker declares February Packers month," *Journal Sentinel* (Milwaukee), February 7, 2011, http://www.jsonline.com/ blogs/news/115504199.html#!page=1&pageSize=10&sort=newestfirst.
3. Paul Breer, "Wisconsin Gov. Walker Threatens to Deploy National Guard as 'Intimidation Force' Against Workers' Unions," ThinkProgress, February 14, 2011, http://thinkprogress.org/economy/2011/02/14/173 785/walker-anti-union-bill/?mobile=nc.
4. Lila Shapiro, "Wisconsin Governor Threatens to Replace Union Work-ers with National Guard," HuffingtonPost.com, February 15, 2011, http://www.huffingtonpost.com/2011/02/15/wisconsin-state-workers -p_n_823476.html.
5. Laura Clawson, "Students and Packers support Wisconsin public workers," Daily Kos, February 15, 2011, http://www.dailykos.com/ story/2011/02/15/945007/-Students-and-Packers-support-Wisconsin -public-workers.
6. Reid Cherner, "The Huddle: Football News from the NFL," *USA Today*, February 15, 2011.
7. Dave Zirin, "BREAKING NEWS: Packers Captain Charles Woodson Stands with Wisconsin's Workers," *The Nation*, February 20, 2011, http://www.thenation.com/blog/158747/breaking-news-packers-captain -charles-woodson-stands-wisconsins-workers#.
8. Jay Weiner, "Packers player Charles Woodson cheers on Wisconsin pub-lic employees," MinnPost.com, February 21, 2011, http://www.minn post.com/political-agenda/2011/02/packers-player-charles-woodson -cheers-wisconsin-public-employees.
9. Sam Stein, "Gilbert Brown, Famed Green Bay Packer, Urges Wis-consin Voters to Recall Republicans," HuffingtonPost.com, August 9, 2011, http://www.huffingtonpost.com/2011/08/09/gilbert-brown-green -bay-packers-wisconsin-recall_n_922271.html?1312911685.

10. NBPA press release, February 25, 2011, http://www.nbpa.org/press -release/press-release-22511.

11. Ibid.

12. Arash Markazi, "Troy Polamalu: Players have cause," ESPNLosAngeles .com, May 23, 2011, http://sports.espn.go.com/nfl/news/story?id=65 80041.

13. Dave Zirin, "DeMaurice Smith: On an NFL Lockout and Inspiration from Egypt," *The Nation*, February 14, 2011, http://psettle.thenation .dev6.fayze2.com/blogs/dave-zirin?page=0%2C12#.

14. Tom Fitzpatrick, "The Baseball Strike: As Boring as It Is Stupid," *Phoenix New Times*, August 18, 1994.

15. Dave Zirin, "Against All Odds: NFL Players Association Emerges from Lockout as Bruised, Battered Victors," *The Nation*, July 25, 2011, http://www.thenation.com/blog/162260/against-all-odds-nfl-players -association-emerges-lockout-bruised-battered-victors.

16. Brian Frederick, "What Fans Should Take Away from the 2011 NFL Lockout," SportsFans.org, July 25, 2011, http://sportsfans.org/ 2011/07/what-fans-should-take-away-from-the-2011-nfl-lockout/.

17. Don Banks, "With end of NFL lockout at hand, it's time to focus on football again," SportsIllustrated.com, July 24, 2011, http://sports illustrated.cnn.com/2011/writers/don_banks/07/24/NFL.lockout/index .html#ixzz1x7Ab3ty0.

18. Staff writers, "David Stern says NBA will lose $300 million this season," SportingNews.com, October 2010, http://aol.sportingnews.com/ nba/feed/2010-10/nba-labor/story/david-stern-says-nba-will-lose-300 -million-this-season#ixzz1x7BBDlBX.

19. Etan Thomas, "NBA labor-negotiation questions," ESPN.com, November 12, 2011, http://espn.go.com/espn/commentary/story/_/id/72 23340/etan-thomas-questions-nba-labor-negotiations.

20. Scoop Jackson, "NBA lockout: A call to *in*action," ESPN.com, October 24, 2011, http://espn.go.com/espn/commentary/story/_/page/jackson -111024/nba-players-write-entire-season.

21. Aaron Kuriloff and Darrell Preston, "Super Bowl Lands on Taxpayers' Backs as Indianapolis Stadium Deal Sours," Bloomberg, February 2, 2012, http://www.bloomberg.com/news/2012-02-02/super-bowl-lands -on-taxpayers-backs-as-stadium-deal-turns-sour.html.

22. Nancy Guyott, "News Release: AFL-CIO Statement on Super Bowl," February 2, 2012, http://in.aflcio.org/statefed/index.cfm?action=article &articleID=edafdab7-98fe-4e5c-a3e9-6b7b2d494ad6.

2: "YOU HAVE TO BE AN ULTRA FROM WITHIN": SOCCER AND THE ARAB SPRING

1. Malika Bilal, "Egypt's 'Ultras' pitch in at Tahrir protest," AlJazeera .com, November 29, 2011, http://www.aljazeera.com/indepth/features/ 2011/11/201111284912960586.html.
2. Sherif Tarek, "Egypt's Ultras: Politically involved but not politically driven, yet," Ahram Online, January16, 2012, http://english.ahram.org .eg/NewsContent/1/64/31904/Egypt/Politics-/Egypt%E2%80%99s-Ultras -Politically-involved-but-not-politi.aspx.
3. Malika Bilal, "Egypt's 'Ultras' pitch in at Tahrir protest," AlJazeera .com, November 29, 2011, http://www.aljazeera.com/indepth/features/ 2011/11/201111284912960586.html.
4. James Montague, "Egypt's revolutionary soccer ultras: How football fans toppled Mubarak," CNN.com, June 29, 2011, http://edition.cnn .com/2011/SPORT/football/06/29/football.ultras.zamalek.ahly/index .html.
5. Ibid.
6. Dave Zirin, "Soccer clubs central to ending Egypt's 'Dictatorship of Fear,'" SportsIllustrated.com, January 31, 2011, http://sportsillustrated .cnn.com/2011/writers/dave_zirin/01/31/egypt.soccer/index.html#ixzz 1x7GM5UT1.
7. Ibid.
8. Wayne Drehs, "The crucible in Cairo," ESPN The Magazine, May 18, 2012.
9. James Dorsey, "Soccer Fans Play Key Role in Egyptian Protests," Turbulent World of Middle East Soccer, January 27, 2011, http://mideast soccer.blogspot.com/2011/01/soccer-fans-play-key-role-in-egyptian.html.
10. James Montague, "Ugly state of the beautiful game in Egypt," The National, February 3, 2012, http://www.thenational.ae/news/world/ middle-east/ugly-state-of-the-beautiful-game-in-egypt.
11. Tarek, "Egypt's Ultras."
12. Ashraf el-Sherif, "The Ultras' Politics of Fun Confront Tyranny," Jadaliyya.com, February 5, 2012, http://www.jadaliyya.com/pages/index/ 4243/the-ultras-politics-of-fun-confront-tyranny-.
13. Dave Zirin, "2011: When Sports Met the World," New Yorker, December 22, 2011, http://www.newyorker.com/online/blogs/newsdesk/ 2011/12/2011-when-sports-met-the-world.html.
14. James Montague, "Egypt's revolutionary soccer ultras: How football fans toppled Mubarak," CNN.com, June 29, 2011, http://edition.cnn .com/2011/SPORT/football/06/29/football.ultras.zamalek.ahly/index .html.

15. James Dorsey, "Egypt suspends soccer matches in anticipation of protest anniversary clashes with ultras," *Turbulent World of Middle East Soccer*, January 22, 2012, http://mideastsoccer.blogspot.com/2012/01/egypt-suspends-soccer-matches-in.html.
16. Tamer Mohamed, "Fuss over sports after Egypt revolt," *Egyptian Gazette*, June 7, 2012, http://213.158.162.45/~egyptian/index.php?action=news&id=23019&title=Fuss%20over%20sports%20after%20Egypt%20revolt.
17. Abdel-Rahman Hussein, "Egypt football match violence: dozens dead and hundreds injured," TheGuardian.co.uk, February 1, 2012, http://www.guardian.co.uk/world/2012/feb/01/egypt-football-match-violence-dead.
18. David D. Kirkpatrick, "Egyptian Soccer Riot Kills More Than 70," *New York Times*, February 1, 2012, http://www.nytimes.com/2012/02/02/world/middleeast/scores-killed-in-egyptian-soccer-mayhem.html.
19. James Dorsey, "Ultras and the Military: Dangerous Games," *al-Akhbar English*, February 3, 2012, http://english.al-akhbar.com/content/ultras-and-military-dangerous-games.
20. James Dorsey, "Port Said blow boosts youth, soccer demands for civilian rule in Egypt," *Middle East Online*, February 4, 2012, http://www.middle-east-online.com/english/?id=50444.
21. Statement from the Revolutionary Socialists, "In defence of the Ultras: their message and our response—Egyptian Revolutionary Socialists on the football stadium massacre," InternationalViewpoint.org, February 2012, http://www.internationalviewpoint.org/spip.php?page=print_article&id_article=2498.
22. "Terminate the Ultras with extreme prejudice," *Whispers from a Seeker*, February 2, 2012, http://perfectionatic.blogspot.com/2012/02/terminate-ultras-with-extreme-prejudice.html.
23. Ibid.
24. Yolande Knell, "Blame game over Egypt's football clashes," BBC News, February 2, 2012, http://www.bbc.co.uk/news/mobile/world-middle-east-16864901.
25. James M. Dorsey, "Port Said helps forge bridges and reopens fault lines in Egypt," *Turbulent World of Middle East Soccer*, http://mideastsoccer.blogspot.com/2012/02/port-said-helps-forge-bridges-and.html.
26. Simeon Kerr and Lina Saigol, "Manama blames foreign interference for unrest," *Financial Times*, March 31, 2011.
27. Dan Murphy, "For Bahrain's soccer team, shades of Saddam Hussein's Iraq," *Christian Science Monitor*, November 10, 2011, http://www.csmonitor.com/World/Backchannels/2011/1110/For-Bahrain-s-soccer-team-shades-of-Saddam-Hussein-s-Iraq.

28. Editorial staff, "Bahrain's soccer stars tortured in custody," *Australian Times*, July 9, 2011, http://www.theaustralian.com.au/news/world/bahrains-soccer-stars-tortured-in-custody/story-e6frg6so-122609091 3602.

29. Michael Casey, "Bahraini Football Brothers Pay the Price for Anti-Regime Demonstration," *Jakarta Globe*, August 31, 2011, http://www.thejakartaglobe.com/football/bahraini-football-brothers-pay-the-price-for-anti-regime-demonstration/462610.

30. Ibid.

31. Staff writers, "Bahrain players banned," ESPN.com, April 7, 2011, http://soccernet.espn.go.com/news/story/_/id/903928/bahrain-players-banned-for-role-in-protests?cc=5901.

3: TODAY'S WORLD CUP AND OLYMPICS: *INVICTUS* IN REVERSE

1. Tom Phillips, "Rio World Cup demolitions leave favela families trapped in ghost town," *Guardian*, April 26, 2011, http://www.guardian.co.uk/world/2011/apr/26/favela-ghost-town-rio-world-cup.

2. Ibid.

3. Ibid.

4. Simon Romero, "Slum Dwellers Are Defying Brazil's Grand Design for Olympics," *New York Times*, March 4, 2012, http://www.nytimes.com/2012/03/05/world/americas/brazil-faces-obstacles-in-preparations-for-rio-olympics.html?_r=1&hp.

5. Editorial staff, "Victory caps hotly contested race," *New York Times*, July 6, 2005, http://www.nytimes.com/2005/07/06/sports/06iht-web.0706olywinner.html.

6. Dave Zirin, *Welcome to the Terrordome: The Pain, Politics, and Promise of Sports* (Chicago: Haymarket Books, 2007).

7. Minky Worden, *China's Great Leap: The Beijing Games and Olympian Human Rights Challenges* (New York: Seven Stories Press, 2008).

8. Ibid.

9. Paul Bedard, "Threat of Shooter at London Olympics a Realistic Possibility," *Washington Examiner*, May 29, 2012, http://washingtonexaminer.com/politics/washington-secrets/2012/05/threat-london-olympics-shooter-realistic-possibility/665956.

10. Juliet Macur and Eric Pfanner, "London Rioting Prompts Fears over Soccer and Olympics," *New York Times*, August 9, 2011, http://www.nytimes.com/2011/08/10/sports/london-rioting-prompts-fears-over-soccer-matches-and-the-olympics.html.

11. China Miéville, "Oh, London, You Drama Queen," *New York Times*

Magazine, March 1, 2012, http://www.nytimes.com/2012/03/04/mag azine/china-mieville-london.html?pagewanted=all.

12. Ibid.

13. Dave Zirin, "The London Olympics and the London Riots," *The Nation*, August 12, 2011, http://www.thenation.com/blog/162742/london -olympics-and-london-riots.

14. Ibid.

15. Andrew Sparrow, "Len McCluskey: unions should consider disrupting London Olympics," *Guardian*, February 28, 2012, http://www.guardian .co.uk/politics/2012/feb/28/len-mccluskey-unions-london-olympics.

16. Greg Bishop, "Vancouver's Former Mayor Remains Face of the Games," *New York Times*, January 1, 2010, http://www.nytimes.com/ 2010/01/31/sports/olympics/31sullivan.html?pagewanted=all.

17. Doug Ward, "Support for Olympics on the decline in B.C.: poll," *Vancouver Sun*, January 21, 2010.

18. Simon Kuper, "The World Cup is no economic boon for South Africa," *Financial Times*, November 28, 2009, http://www.ft.com/intl/cms/ s/0/2911d7f6-dbbd-11de-9424-00144feabdc0.html#axzz1x7TYE4gb.

19. Oliver Harvey, "Homeless and Away," *The Sun*, April 19, 2010, http:// www.thesun.co.uk/sol/homepage/features/2936217/Tin-Can-Town-next -to-South-Africa-World-Cup-stadium.html.

20. David Smith, "Life in 'Tin Can Town' for the South Africans evicted ahead of World Cup," *Guardian*, April 1, 2010, http://www.guardian .co.uk/world/2010/apr/01/south-africa-world-cup-blikkiesdorp.

21. Sapa, "Mpumalanga ANC distances itself from hit list," Politics Web, February 10, 2010, http://www.politicsweb.co.za/politicsweb/view/ politicsweb/en/page71619?oid=159819&sn=Detail.

22. Daniel Bloom and Dave Zirin, "World Cup Hangover Hits South Africa," *The Nation*, September 14, 2010, http://www.thenation.com/ article/154706/world-cup-hangover-hits-south-africa#.

23. Barry Bearak, "Cost of Stadium Reveals Tensions in South Africa," *New York Times*, March 12, 2010.

24. http://en.wikiquote.org/wiki/Leymah_Gbowee.

25. Kate Griffiths, "1.3 Million Public Workers Strike to Confront South Africa's Inequalities," Labor Notes, September 8, 2010, http://labor notes.org/2010/09/13-million-public-workers-strike-confront-south -africas-inequalities.

4: ZOMBIE TEAMS AND ZOMBIE OWNERS

1. Joe Flint, "Dodgers sale could mean bigger cable bills," *Los Angeles Times*, March 28, 2012, http://latimesblogs.latimes.com/entertain

mentnewsbuzz/2012/03/dodgers-sale-could-mean-bigger-cable-bills
.html.

2. National Public Radio, "Michigan Gov.: Job Loss 'Our Own Katrina.'" March 17, 2009, http://www.npr.org/templates/story/story.php
?storyId=101990867.

3. Neil deMause, "Why Do Mayors Love Sports Stadiums?" *The Nation*, August 15, 2011, http://www.thenation.com/article/162400/
why-do-mayors-love-sports-stadiums.

4. National Football League, "Goodell: 'We can and will reach an agreement' on CBA," NFL.com, January 3, 2011, http://www.nfl.com/news/
story/09000d5d81d6d8e0/article/goodell-we-can-and-will-reach-an
-agreement-on-cba-.

5. Associated Press, "Pirates made $29.4M in 2007 and 2008," ESPN
.com, August 23, 2010, http://sports.espn.go.com/mlb/news/story?id
=5484947.

6. Jeff Passan, "Marlins' Profits Came at Taxpayer Expense," Yahoo! Sports,
August 24, 2010, http://sports.yahoo.com/mlb/news?slug=jp-marlins
financials082410.

7. Patrick Hruby, "Time to 'Occupy the Marlins,'" Yahoo! Sports, December 13, 2011, http://www.thepostgame.com/commentary/201112/
hruby-tuesday-miami-marlins-occupy-mlb.

8. Ted Leonsis, "Class Warfare—Yuck!" *Ted's Take*, September 25, 2011,
http://www.tedstake.com/2011/09/25/class-warfare-yuck/.

9. Malcolm Gladwell, "The Nets and NBA Economics," *Grantland*,
September 26, 2011, http://www.grantland.com/story/_/id/7021031/
the-nets-nba-economics.

10. Michael David Smith, "Goodell tells fans lockout is for them,
too," NBC Sports, June 9, 2011, http://profootballtalk.nbcsports
.com/2011/06/09/goodell-tells-fans-lockout-is-for-them-too/.

11. Sally Jenkins, "NFL lockout: Owners get the keys to stadiums, fans
get the bills," *Washington Post*, March 15, 2011.

12. Abbie Boudreau and Scott Shulman, "Los Angeles Dodgers Owner
Frank McCourt Speaks Out About Divorce Drama," *Good Morning
America*, May 5, 2011, http://abcnews.go.com/US/los-angeles-dodgers
-owner-frank-mccourt-speaks-divorce/story?id=13532508#.T9DqC4
74m0o.

13. Harold Meyerson, "The L.A. Dodgers fall prey to CEO capitalism run
amok," *Washington Post*, June 28, 2011, http://www.washingtonpost
.com/opinions/the-la-dodgers-fall-prey-to-ceo-capitalism-run-amok/
2011/06/28/AGG9kmpH_story.html.

14. http://thinkexist.com/quotation/as_one_went_to_europe_to_see_the
_living_past-so/222692.html.

15. Meyerson, "The L.A. Dodgers fall prey."

16. Barry Petchesky, "How Bernie Madoff's Money Ran the Mets," Dead-
    spin, February 21, 2012, http://deadspin.com/5886867/how-bernie
    -madoffs-money-ran-the-mets.

17. Adam Rubin, "Wilpons issue statement," ESPN, February 4, 2011,
    http://espn.go.com/blog/new-yorkmets/post/_/id/13926/wilpons-issue
    -statement.

18. Jeff Passan, "Mets' problems go beyond Castillo, Perez," Yahoo Sports,
    March 23, 2011, http://sports.yahoo.com/mlb/news?slug=jp-passan
    _mets_scandal_ownership_wilpon_katz_madoff_picard_selig_032311

19. Dave Zirin, "Those Non-Profit Packers," New Yorker, January 25, 2011,
    http://www.newyorker.com/online/blogs/sportingscene/2011/01/those
    -non-profit-packers.html.

20. KTLA, "Councilwoman Proposes Public Ownership of Dodgers,"
    http://janicehahn.com/coverage/councilwoman-proposes-public-owner
    ship-of-dodgers/.

5: JOE PATERNO: DEATH, REMEMBRANCE, AND THE WAGES OF SIN

1. Aurin Squire, "Paterno, Piety and Penn State: The Conversation No
   One Wants," Bleacher Report, November 10, 2011, http://bleacher
   report.com/articles/935185-paterno-piety-and-penn-state-the-conver
   sation-no-one-wants.

2. Sally Jenkins, "Joe Paterno's last interview," Washington Post, January 13, 2012, http://www.washingtonpost.com/sports/colleges/joe-paternos
   -first-interview-since-the-penn-state-sandusky-scandal/2012/01/13/gI
   QA08e4yP_print.html.

3. "Thousands gather at Joe Paterno tribute," Associated Press, January 27, 2012, http://espn.go.com/college-football/story/_/id/7506640/
   joe-paterno-penn-state-nittany-lions-memorial-exposes-anger-firing.

4. See the anti-sweatshop work of former St. John's soccer coach Jim
   Keady: http://www.teamsweat.org/tag/jim-keady/.

5. Jessica Bennett and Jacob Bernstein, "Penn State Football's Economic
   Clout," Daily Beast, November 24, 2011, http://www.thedailybeast
   .com/articles/2011/11/24/the-power-of-penn-state-football-s-economic
   -clout.html.

6. Jonathan Mahler, Death Comes to Happy Valley: Penn State and the
   Tragic Legacy of Joe Paterno (San Francisco: Byliner, 2012).

7. Peter King, "Monday Morning Quarterback," Sports Illustrated, November 14, 2011, http://sportsillustrated.cnn.com/2011/writers/peter
   _king/11/14/Week10/1.html.

8. Ivan Maisel, "Joe Paterno: I met my responsibilities," ESPN, Novem-

ber 7, 2011, http://espn.go.com/college-football/story/_/id/7200340/
joe-paterno-penn-state-nittany-lions-says-true-were-all-fooled.

9. Dave Zirin, "The World Joe Paterno Made," *The Nation*, November 14, 2011, http://www.thenation.com/blog/164587/world-joe-paterno
-made.

10. Nathan Ferno, "At Penn State's stadium, profanity, scorn greet one father's protest," *Washington Times*, November 12, 2011.

11. Ibid.

12. Dick Weiss, "JoePa haunted by past decision made at PSU," *Daily News*, November 10, 2011, http://articles.nydailynews.com/2011-11-10/
news/30379950_1_joe-paterno-sexual-assault-sexual-misconduct/2.

13. Associated Press, "NOW leader calls for Paterno's resignation," January 8, 2006, http://sports.espn.go.com/ncf/news/story?id=2284993.

14. Reed Albergotti, "A Discipline Problem," *Wall Street Journal*, November 22, 2011, http://online.wsj.com/article/SB1000142405297020444
34045770520736725614f02.html?mod=ITP_pageone_0.

15. Staff report, "Nebraska coach Bo Pelini says game vs. Penn State shouldn't have been played," *Sporting News*, November 14, 2011, /
ncaa-football/story/2011-11-14/nebraska-coach-bo-pelini-says-game-vs
-penn-state-shouldnt-have-been-played.

6: THE NCAA'S "WHIFF OF THE PLANTATION"

1. These data derive from a margin note in a hard copy of *Sports Illustrated* that, alas, I have misplaced.

2. Associated Press, "NCAA Report: Economy Cuts Into Sports," ESPN
.com, August 23, 2010, http://sports.espn.go.com/ncf/news/story?id
=5490686.

3. Steve Berkowitz and Jodi Upton, "Salaries rising for new college football coaches," *USA Today*, January 16, 2012, http://www.usatoday
.com/sports/college/football/story/2012-01-16/College-football-coaches
-compenstion/52602734/1.

4. Steve Wieberg, "NCAA president: Time to discuss players getting sliver of revenue pie," *USA Today*, March 29, 2011, http://www.usatoday
.com/sports/college/mensbasketball/2011-03-29-ncaa-pay-for-play
-final-four_N.htm?sms_ss=gmail&at_xt=4d93d876081f62dd,0%22.

5. *Frontline*, "Money and March Madness", PBS, March 29, 2011, http://
www.pbs.org/wgbh/pages/frontline/money-and-march-madness/inter
views/mark-emmert.html.

6. Editorial staff, "NCAA President Says He's Ready to Explore Increasing Financial Aid for Athletes," *Frontline*, March 30, 2011, http://www
.pbs.org/wgbh/pages/frontline/2011/03/ncaa-president-says-hes-ready
-to-explore-paying-athletes.html.

7. Taylor Branch, "The Shame of College Sports," *The Atlantic*, October 2011, http://www.theatlantic.com/magazine/archive/2011/10/the-shame-of-college-sports/8643/.
8. Laura Pappano, "How Big-Time Sports Ate College Life," *New York Times*, January 20, 2012, http://www.nytimes.com/2012/01/22/education/edlife/how-big-time-sports-ate-college-life.html?pagewanted=all.
9. *Frontline*, "Money and March Madness."
10. Branch, "The Shame of College Sports."
11. Michael McCarthy, "ESPN's Desmond Howard rips 'wicked' college system," *USA Today*, July 29, 2011, http://content.usatoday.com/communities/gameon/post/2011/07/espns-desmond-howard-says-wicked-college-system-exploitive-of-players/1#.T9ESNhyZdqw.
12. Branch, "The Shame of College Sports."
13. Ibid.
14. Ibid.
15. Ibid.
16. Jalen Rose, "Paid College Athletes: A Reasonable Compromise," Huffington Post, March 16, 2011, http://www.huffingtonpost.com/jalen-rose/paid-college-athletes-a-r_b_836449.html.
17. George Fitzhugh, *Cannibals All! or, Slaves Without Masters* (Richmond, VA: A. Morris, 1857).
18. Dave D'Alessandro, "Terrelle Pryor faces a double standard with NFL," *Star-Ledger* (New Jersey), August 17, 2011, http://www.nj.com/giants/index.ssf/2011/08/dalessandro_terrelle_pryor_fac.html.
19. Greg Bishop, "E. Gordon Gee's Not-So Greatest Hits," *The Quad*, *New York Times*, August 13, 2011, http://thequad.blogs.nytimes.com/2011/08/13/e-gordon-gees-not-so-greatest-hits/.
20. Editorial staff, "Ex-PSU assistants to get $4.4 M in severance," CBS Sports, January 20, 2012, http://www.cbssports.com/collegefootball/story/16944670/expsu-assistants-to-get-44-m-in-severance.
21. Ralph K. M. Haurwitz, "Mack Brown's salary deemed 'unseemly,'" *Austin American-Statesman*, http://www.statesman.com/news/texas/mack-browns-salary-deemed-unseemly-121287.html.
22. Edwin Bear, "Texas Head Coach Mack Brown Deserves His Two Million Dollar Raise," Bleacher Report, December 16, 2009, http://bleacherreport.com/articles/309786-texas-head-coach-mack-brown-deserves-his-two-million-dollar-raise.
23. Haurwitz, "Mack Brown's salary deemed 'unseemly.'"
24. Branch, "The Shame of College Sports."

7: HERE COME LOS SUNS

1. "Rep. Kyrsten Sinema explains her opposition to Republicans' birther bill on House floor," video at http://www.democraticunderground.com/discuss/duboard.php?az=view_all&address=385x457981.

2. Tom Krattenmaker, *Onward Christian Athletes: Turning Ballparks into Pulpits and Players into Preachers* (Lanham, MD: Rowman & Littlefield Publishers, 2009), 134.

3. Lindsay Goldwert, "John McCain: Illegal immigrants are intentionally causing car accidents," *Daily News*, April 20, 2010, http://articles.nydailynews.com/2010-04-20/news/27062225_1_illegal-immigrants-john-mccain-car-accidents.

4. Dave Zirin, "Diamondbacks Owner Ken Kendrick Continues to Support SB 1070," *The Nation*, May 10, 2010.

5. Dave Zirin, "To Catch a Fire: Diamondback Protests Take Off," Huffington Post, April 29, 2010, http://www.huffingtonpost.com/dave-zirin/to-catch-a-fire-diamondba_b_557130.html.

6. Dave Zirin, "'Today We Did Some Good': The Diamondbacks Demonstration in DC," *The Nation*, August 16, 2010, http://www.thenation.com/blog/154049/today-we-did-some-good-diamondbacks-demonstration-dc.

7. ESPN Wire Services, "Sheffield says Latin players easier to control than blacks," ESPN, June 3, 2007, http://sports.espn.go.com/mlb/news/story?id=2891875.

8. Dave Zirin, "Pressure Builds on Bud Selig to Move 2011 All-Star Game," *The Progressive*, http://www.progressive.org/node/142107/80361.

9. Ibid.

10. Ibid.

11. Ibid.

12. Scott Boeck, "D'Backs, union have concerns about Arizona's new immigration laws," *USA Today*, April 30, 2010, http://content.usatoday.com/communities/dailypitch/post/2010/04/mlbpa-executive-director-weiner-does-not-support-arizonas-immigration-law/1#.T9FvSo74m0.

13. Paul Coro, "Phoenix to wear 'Los Suns' jerseys for Game 2 vs. Spurs," *Arizona Republic*, May 4, 2010, http://www.azcentral.com/sports/suns/articles/2010/05/04/20100504phoenix-suns-los-suns-jerseys.html.

14. Ibid.

15. Steve Krakauer, "Phoenix NBA Team to Make Political Statement with 'Los Suns' Uniform Tonight," Mediaite, May 5, 2010, http://www.mediaite.com/online/phoenix-nba-team-to-make-political-statement-with-los-suns-uniform-tonight/.

16. Dave Zirin, "Boycott Phil Jackson: Why Lakers Fans Should Root for

Los Suns," *The Nation*, May 16, 2010, http://www.thenation.com/blog/boycott-phil-jackson-why-lakers-fans-should-root-los-suns.

17. Edgar Collie, "Are you willing to speak up in Dallas Texas?" *The Examiner*, http://www.examiner.com/article/are-you-willing-to-speak-up-dallas-texas.

18. Jim Galloway, "With Sunday sales and immigration, Georgia's center of gravity shifts to suburbia," *Atlanta Journal-Constitution*, April 16, 2011, http://blogs.ajc.com/political-insider-jim-galloway/2011/04/16/with-sunday-sales-and-immigration-georgias-center-of-gravity-shifts-to-suburbia/.

19. Gregg Doyel, "Embattled Arizona doesn't deserve hate, boycotts," CBS Sports, http://www.cbssports.com/mlb/story/13368448/embattled-arizona-doesnt-deserve-hate-boycotts.

20. Media Matters for America, "Kristol Misrepresents Phoenix Crime Levels to Defend AZ Law," July 2, 2010, http://mediamatters.org/research/201007020014.

21. Craig Calcaterra, "Sheriff Joe Arpaio to use the All-Star Game to draw attention to himself," NBC Sports, July 8, 2011, http://hardballtalk.nbcsports.com/2011/07/08/sheriff-joe-arpaio-to-use-the-all-star-game-to-draw-attention-to-himself/.

22. Julianne Hing, "To Protest Arizona's SB 1070 or Play in Tonight's All-Star Game?," Colorlines, July 12 2011, http://colorlines.com/archives/2011/07/to_protest_arizonas_sb_1070_or_play_in_tonights_all-star_game.html.

8: "IS YOUR UNDERWEAR FLAME RETARDANT?" SEXUALITY AND SPORTS

1. Elizabeth Schulte, "Sparks of a new women's movement," *Socialist Worker*, http://socialistworker.org/2011/05/17/a-new-womens-movement.

2. Tucker Center, "Double Standards: Portrayals of Female Athletes in Mainstream Sports Media," September 22, 2009, http://tuckercenter.wordpress.com/2009/09/22/131/.

3. Allison Glock, "The Selling of Candace Parker," *ESPN The Magazine*, http://sports.espn.go.com/espnmag/story?id=3967891.

4. Sportsmail Reporter, "World champion Caster Semenya 'is a hermaphrodite with no womb or ovaries,'" *Daily Mail*, http://www.dailymail.co.uk/sport/othersports/article-1212568/World-champion-Caster-Semenya-hermaphrodite-womb-ovaries—Australian-newspapers-shock-claims-gender-row-runner.html.

5. Intersex Society of North America, "How common is intersex?," http://www.isna.org/faq/frequency.

6. Genetics Home Reference, "Androgen insensitivity syndrome," July 2, 2012, http://ghr.nlm.nih.gov/condition/androgen-insensitivity-syndrome.
7. Sherry Wolf, *Sexuality and Socialism* (Chicago: Haymarket Books, 2009).
8. Tommy Craggs, "Caster Semenya Is a 'Hermaphrodite,' Ballsy Aussie PaperReports,"Deadspin,http://deadspin.com/5356717/caster-semenya-is-a-hermaphrodite-ballsy-aussie-paper-reports.
9. Pumza Fihlani, "Crowds greet gender-test athlete," BBC News, http://news.bbc.co.uk/2/hi/8218530.stm.
10. David Smith, "Caster Semenya row: 'Who are white people to question the makeup of an African girl? It is racism,'" *The Guardian*, http://www.guardian.co.uk/sport/2009/aug/23/caster-semenya-athletics-gender.
11. Rebecca Jordan-Young and Katrina Karkazis, "You Say You're a Woman? That Should Be Enough," *New York Times*, June 17, 2012, http://www.nytimes.com/2012/06/18/sports/olympics/olympic-sex-verification-you-say-youre-a-woman-that-should-be-enough.html?ref=sports&gwh=41EBC2FF66D7EC3016FB8C68D4B478CD.
12. Molly Jay, *Winning Woman: 500 Spirited Quotes About Women and Their Sport* (Philadelphia: Running Press, 2001), 199.
13. Larry Schwartz, Didrikson was a woman ahead of her time, http://espn.go.com/sportscentury/features/00014147.html
14. Paul Lukas, "From Corsets to Catsuits," ESPN.com, http://sports.espn.go.com/espn/page2/story?page=lukas/050620.
15. Susan K. Cahn, *Coming On Strong: Gender and Sexuality in Twentieth-Century Women's Sports* (Cambridge, MA: Harvard University Press, 1998).
16. Ibid.
17. Ibid.
18. Ibid.
19. Ibid.
20. Ibid.
21. Larry Schwartz, "Billie Jean won for all women," ESPN, January 1, 2000, http://espn.go.com/sportscentury/features/00016060.html.
22. Ibid.
23. Ibid.
24. Tara Parker-Pope, "As Girls Become Women, Sports Pay Dividends," *New York Times*, February 15, 2010, http://www.nytimes.com/2010/02/16/health/16well.html.
25. *Training Rules*, dir. Dee Mossbacher, Woman Vision, 2009.
26. Randy Boyd, "First Gays, Then Animals, Then More Cock-Teases," Outsports, http://www.outsports.com/ballin/20032004/0721smoltzbonus.htm.

27. Howard Zinn, *A People's History of the United States: 1492–Present* (New York: Harper Perennial Modern Classics, 2003), 283.

28. Tom Farrey, *Game On: How the Pressure to Win at All Costs Endangers Youth Sports and What Parents Can Do About It;* (ESPN Books, 2009) 106

29. Elliott J. Gorn and Warren Goldstein, *A Brief History of American Sports* (Champaign: University of Illinois Press, 2004), 91.

30. Albert G. Spalding, *America's National Game* (New York, 1911), 11.

31. Ann Meredith, "Gay Games II," *Off Our Backs*, October 31, 1986.

32. Ibid.

33. Brendan Ayanbadejo, "Same Sex Marriages: What's the Big Deal?," Huffington Post, April 23, 2009, http://www.huffingtonpost.com/ brendon-ayanbadejo/same-sex-marriages-whats_b_190591.html.

34. Dave Zirin, "'Why I Support the National Equality March': NFL's Scott Fujita Speaks Out for Gay Rights," Edge of Sports Radio, October 2009, http://www.edgeofsports.com/2009-10-06-460/index.html.

35. L. Jon Wertheim, "Gays in Sports: A Poll," *Sports Illustrated*, April 18, 2005, http://sportsillustrated.cnn.com/vault/article/magazine/MAG11 10762/index.htm.

36. Sherry Wolf, "America's Deepest Closet," August 15, 2011, *The Nation*, http://www.thenation.com/article/162386/americas-deepest-closet.

37. Tim Hardaway Foundation press release, "Tim Hardaway Pledges Support for 'No Recall Group,' Gay Issues," August 23, 2011, http://www .thfla.com/2011/08/tim-hardaway-pledges-support-for-no-recall-group -gay-issues/.

38. ESPN.com news services, "Charles Barkley: I had gay teammates," ESPN.com, http://sports.espn.go.com/nba/news/story?id=6563128.

39. Johnette Howard, "The issues in Wayne Simmonds' version," ESPN .com, September 28, 2011, http://espn.go.com/espn/commentary/ story/_/page/howard-110927/wayne-simmonds-alleged-gay-slur-puts -nhl-difficult-position.

40. Tim Murphy, "Focus on the Family Head: 'We've Probably Lost' on Gay Marriage," *Mother Jones*, May 23, 2011, http://www.motherjones .com/mojo/2011/05/focus-family-weve-lost-gay-marriage.

41. Henry Abbott, "David Stern predicts openly gay players," ESPN.com, April 15, 2011, http://espn.go.com/blog/truehoop/post/_/id/27380/ david-stern-predicts-openly-gay-players.

9: "I'M NOT YOUR CHILD": RACISM TODAY IN SPORTS

1. *Outside the Lines*, ESPN.

2. Staff report, "Wade, Stern Have Blow Up at Friday's NBA Labor Meeting," *Sporting News*, September 30, 2011, http://aol.sportingnews.com/

nba/story/2011-09-30/wade-stern-have-blowup-at-fridays-nba-labor
-meeting.
3. Bill Simmons, "Proactively Mourning the NBA," *Grantland*, October21,2011,http://www.grantland.com/story/_/id/7131896/proactively
-mourning-nba.
4. *Not Just a Game*, dir. Jeremy Earp, Media Education Foundation,
2010.
5. Bob Sloan, "Insourcing—Identifying businesses involved in prison
labor or supporting those who are," Daily Kos, December 14, 2010,
http://www.dailykos.com/story/2010/12/14/928611/-INSOURCING
-Identifying-businesses-involved-in-prison-labor-or-supporting-those
-who-are.
6. Dave Zirin, "Michael Vick and the Forgotten Masses," *The Nation*,
August 31, 2011.
7. Michelle Alexander, *The New Jim Crow* (New York City: The New
Press, 2011), 180.
8. Charlene Muhammad, "Corporate greed and private prisons," *Final
Call*,May1,2007,http://www.finalcall.com/artman/publish/article_3440
.shtml.
9. Henry Schulman, "SF Giants' Bochy: Tony Bruno's comment racist,"
San Francisco Chronicle, August 8, 2011, http://www.sfgate.com/cgi
-bin/article.cgi?f=/c/a/2011/08/07/SPSI1KKHH2.DTL.
10. Ben Chew, "Radio host Tony Bruno calls Giants pitcher 'illegal alien'
on Twitter," NBC Sports, August 7, 2011, http://offthebench.nbcsports
.com/2011/08/07/radio-host-tony-bruno-calls-giants-pitcher-illegal-alien
-on-twitter/.
11. Michael Cabanatuan, "Radio host's tweet on SF Giants stirs uproar,"
San Francisco Chronicle, August 7, 2011, http://www.sfgate.com/cgi
-bin/article.cgi?f=/c/a/2011/08/07/SP9N1KKD8D.DTL.
12. Ian Begley, "Floyd Mayweather questions Jeremy Lin," February 14,
2012, ESPN.com, http://espn.go.com/new-york/nba/story/_/id/75726
90/floyd-mayweather-says-new-york-knicks-jeremy-lin-spotlight-race
-not-play.
13. David Lariviere, "Lin putting bounce back in U.S. basketball,"
China Daily, February 18, 2012, http://www.chinadaily.com.cn/
sports/2012-02/18/content_14637340.htm.
14. Charles Pierce, "Our Mr. Brooks Takes It to the Rack," *Esquire*, February 17, 2012, http://www.esquire.com/blogs/politics/david-brooks
-jeremy-lin-6693168.
15. Gene Lyons, "The futile search for meaning in 'Linsanity,' " Salon, February 22, 2012, http://www.salon.com/2012/02/23/the_futile_search
_for_meaning_in_linsanity/.

16. Sean Newell, "ESPN's Headline Writers Join in the Linsanity: 'Chink in the Armor' Edition," Deadspin, February 18, 2012, http://deadspin.com/5886218/espns-headline-writers-join-in-the-linsanity-chink-in-the-armor-edition.
17. Editorial staff, "ESPN Fires Employee for Jeremy Lin Racist Headline," Huffington Post, February 19, 2012, http://www.huffingtonpost.com/2012/02/19/espn-fires-employee-jeremy-lin-headline_n_1287591.html.
18. Benjamin R. Freed, "Bruins Fans React to Joel Ward's Game-Winning Goal with Obscenely Racist Tweets," DCist, April 27, 2012, http://dcist.com/2012/04/racist_boston_fans.php.
19. Greg Wyshynski, "Bruins MVP Tim Thomas skips Obama White House event; why he shouldn't be demonized for it," January 23, 2012, http://sports.yahoo.com/blogs/nhl-puck-daddy/bruins-mvp-tim-thomas-skips-white-house-event-203636656.html.
20. Alex Seitz-Wald, "Glenn Beck Suggests Tea Party Is Racist," Think Progress, December 12, 2011, http://thinkprogress.org/politics/2011/12/12/387451/glenn-beck-suggests-tea-party-is-racist/?mobile=nc.
21. Paul Flannery, "Give Bill Russell a Damn Statue!" Boston, December 2010, http://www.bostonmagazine.com/articles/2010/11/give-bill-russell-a-damn-statue/.

POST-GAME

1. Tony Perry, "Junior Seau's brain will be studied for signs of concussions," Los Angeles Times, May 4, 2012, http://latimesblogs.latimes.com/lanow/2012/05/junior-seaus-brain-will-be-studied-for-signs-of-concussions.html.
2. Jim Trotter, "Remembering Junior: Seau's legacy extends well beyond his NFL feats," Sports Illustrated, May 2, 2012, http://sportsillustrated.cnn.com/2012/writers/jim_trotter/05/02/junior.seau/index.html#ixzz1tnjD7Q8T.
3. Mike Tierney, "Former Player's Suicide Won't End His Widow's Fight," New York Times, May 3, 2012, http://www.nytimes.com/2012/05/04/sports/ray-easterlings-widow-to-keep-fighting-for-retired-nfl-players-with-head-injuries.html?pagewanted=all.
4. Michael David Smith, "Merril Hoge: Kurt Warner is uneducated and irresponsible," NBC Sports, May 4, 2012, http://profootballtalk.nbcsports.com/2012/05/04/merril-hoge-kurt-warner-is-uneducated-and-irresponsible/.
5. Paul Jackiewicz, "Kurt Warner says he loves football, but not the violence," Pro Football Zone, May 7, 2012, http://profootballzone.com/nfl/kurt-warner-says-he-loves-football-but-not-the-violence/.
6. Brandon Marshall, "Brandon Marshall offers his thoughts on Junior

Seau tragedy," *Chicago Sun-Times*, May 5, 2012, http://www.sun times.com/sports/12306507-419/lets-use-junior-seau-tragedy-as-oppor tunity-to-learn.html.

7. Peter Keating, "Heading for Trouble," *ESPN The Magazine*, http:// sports.espn.go.com/espnmag/story?id=3958650.

8. http://sports.yahoo.com/news/nfl—maryland-politician%E2%80%99s -letter-denouncing-brendon-ayanbadejo%E2%80%99s-support-of-gay -marriage.html.

9. http://www.usatoday.com/sports/football/nfl/ravens/story/2012-09-07/ brendan-ayanbadejo-gay-marriage/57680822/1.

10. http://deadspin.com/5941348/they-wont-magically-turn-you-into-a-lust ful-cockmonster-chris-kluwe-explains-gay-marriage-to-the-politician-who -is-offended-by-an-nfl-player-supporting-it?.

Index

Celebrating Independent Publishing

Thank you for reading this book published by The New Press. The New Press is a nonprofit, public interest publisher. New Press books and authors play a crucial role in sparking conversations about the key political and social issues of our day.

We hope you enjoyed this book and that you will stay in touch with The New Press. Here are a few ways to stay up to date with our books, our events, and the issues we cover:

- Sign up at www.thenewpress.com/subscribe to receive updates on New Press authors and issues and to be notified about local events
- Like us on Facebook: www.facebook.com/newpressbooks
- Follow us on Twitter: www.twitter.com/thenewpress

Please consider buying New Press books for yourself; for friends and family; or to donate to schools, libraries, community centers, prison libraries, and other organizations involved with the issues our authors write about.

The New Press is a 501(c)(3) nonprofit organization. You can also support our work with a tax-deductible gift by visiting www.thenewpress.com/donate.